Animal Kingdom

Stress Relieving Patterns and Designs

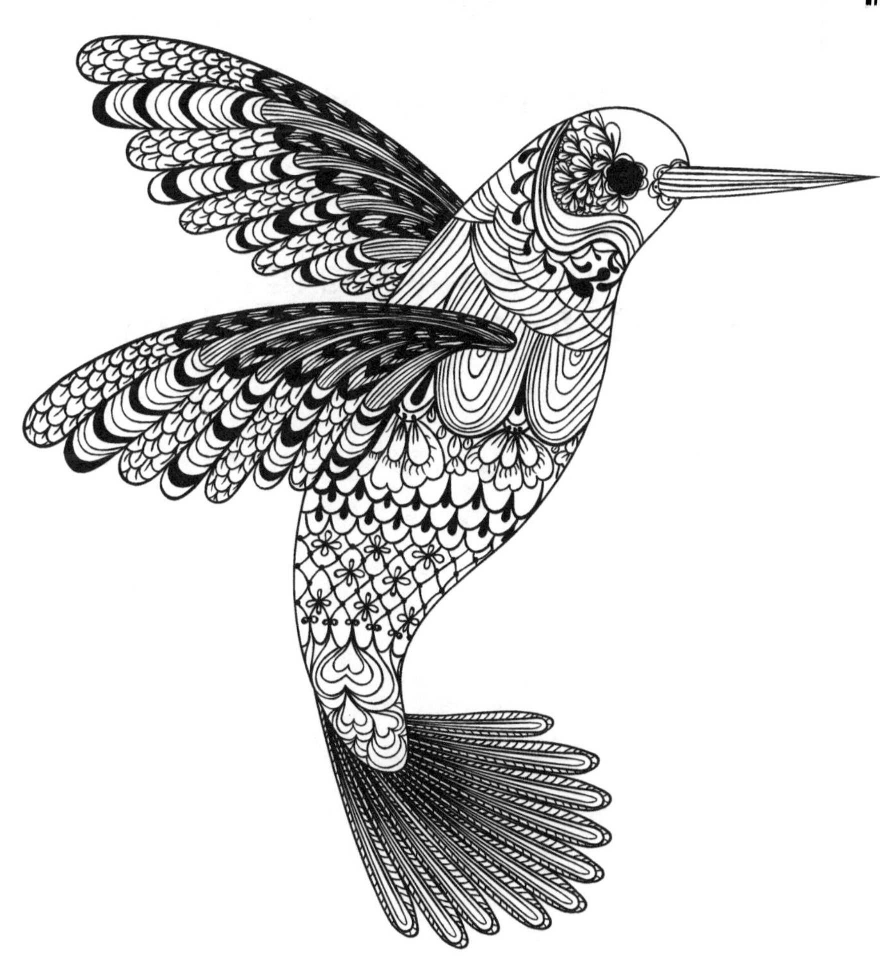

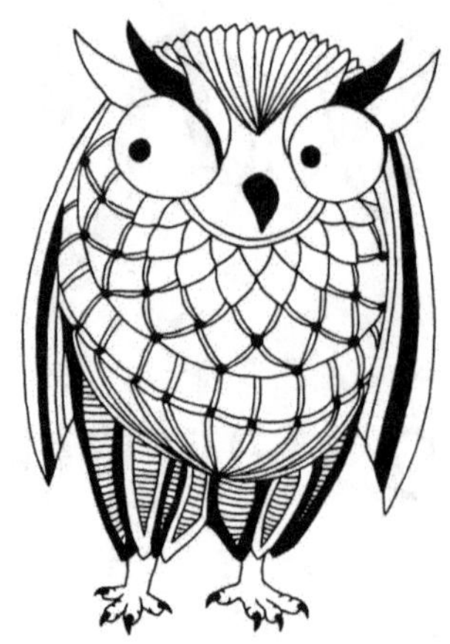

At COLOR and DOODLE, we believe that coloring is GOOD for the SOUL.

So relax and be creative!

Download free coloring pages at
www.ColorandDoodle.com

Color and Doodle Publishing
1684 Decoto Rd
Union City, CA 94587

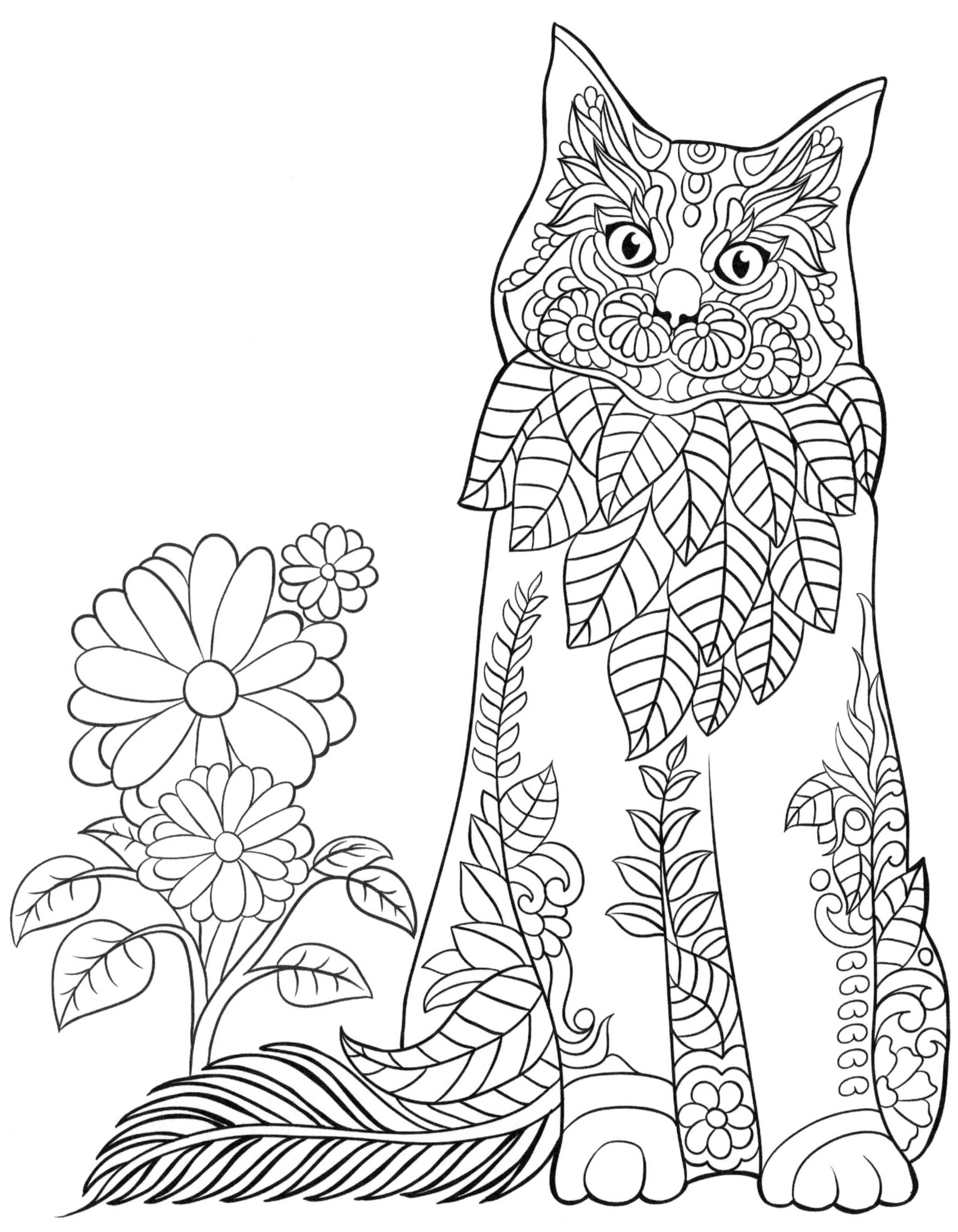

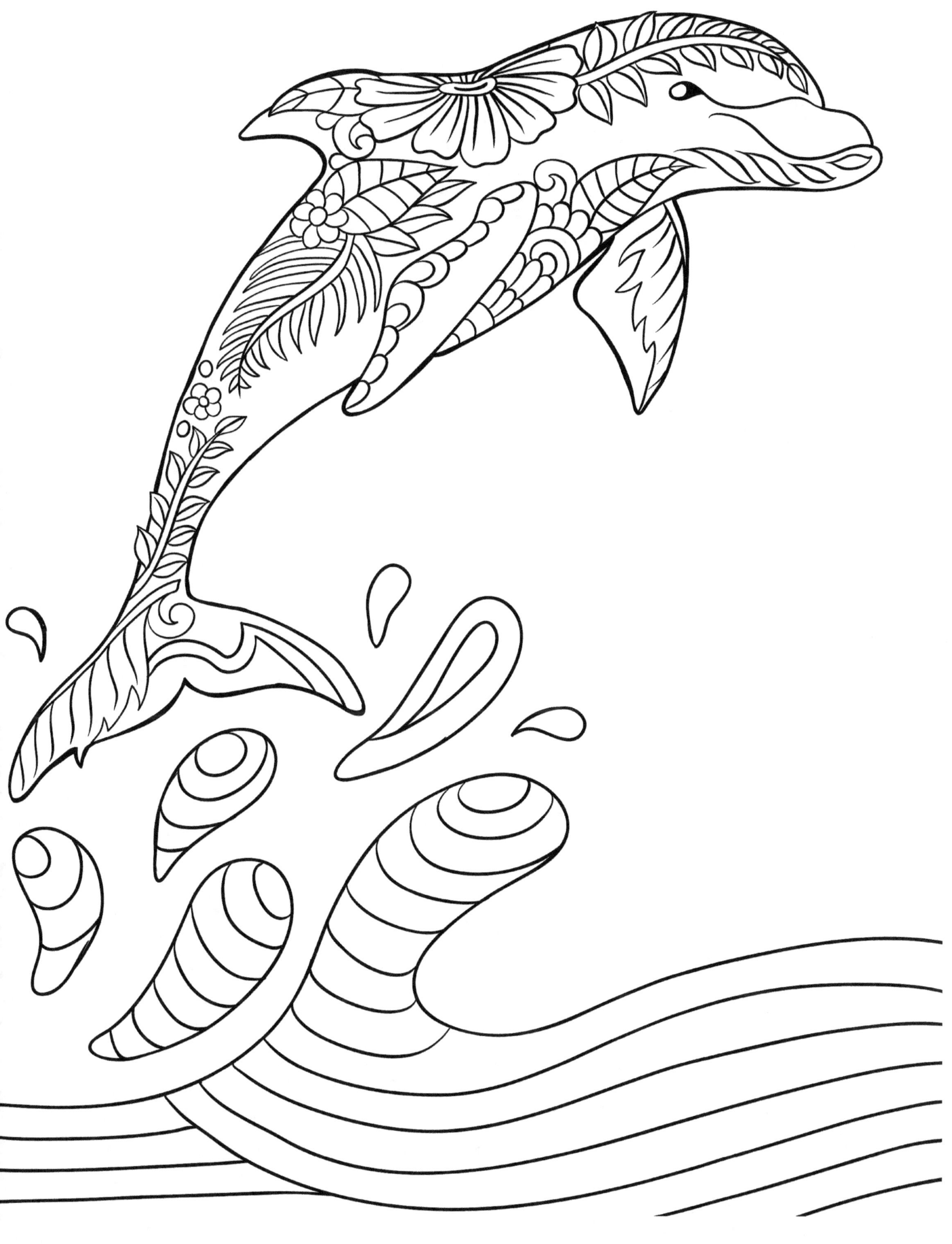

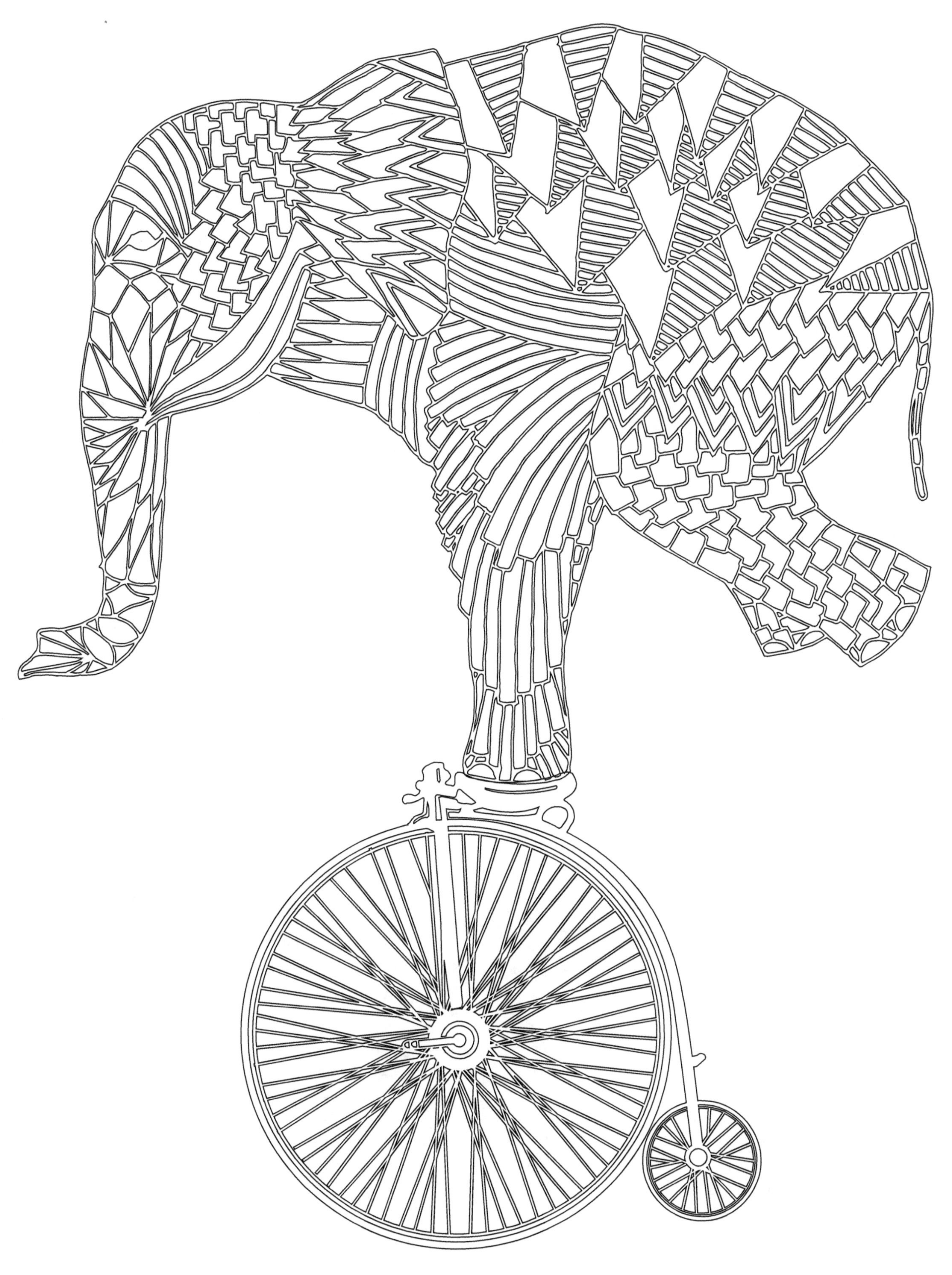

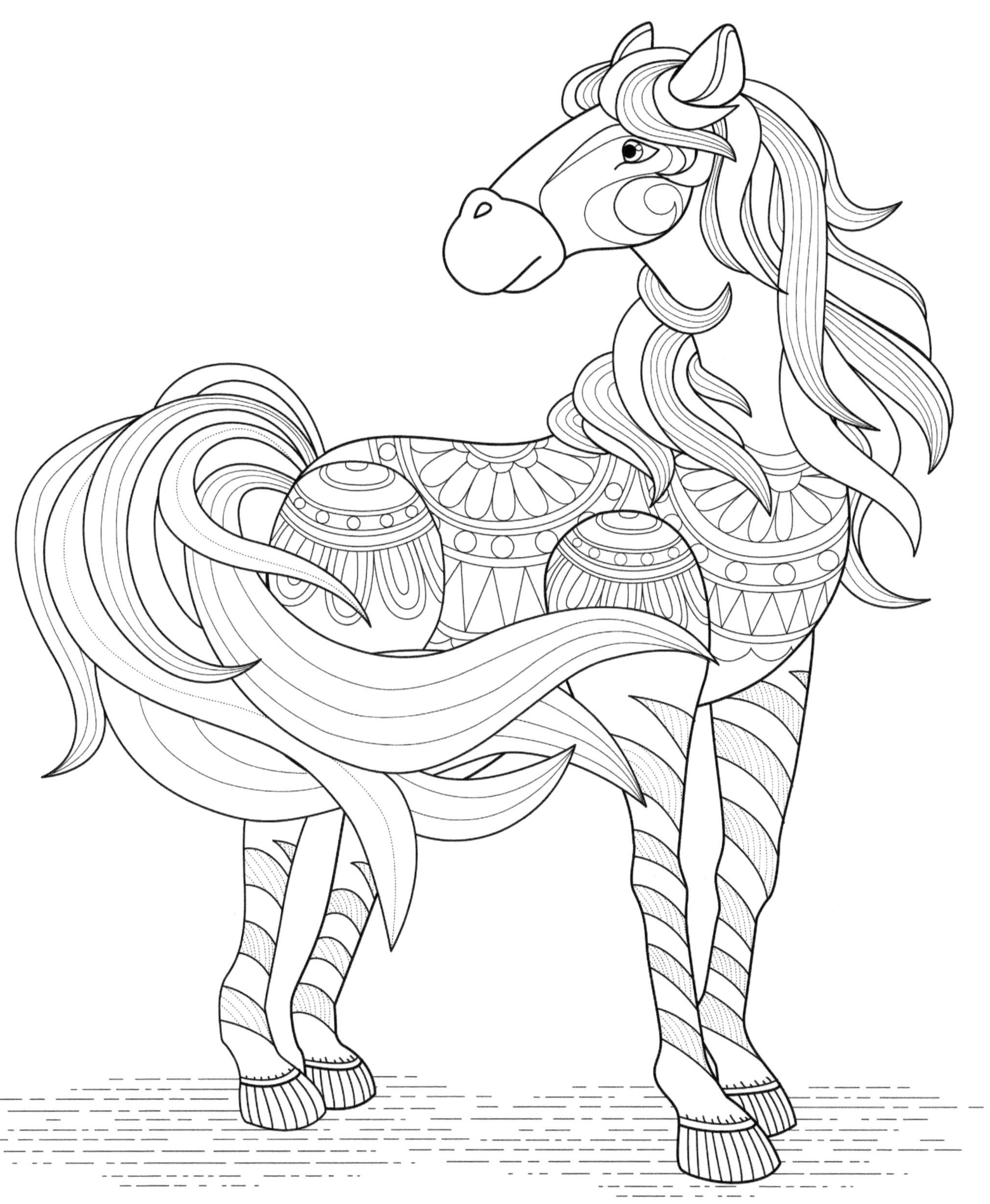

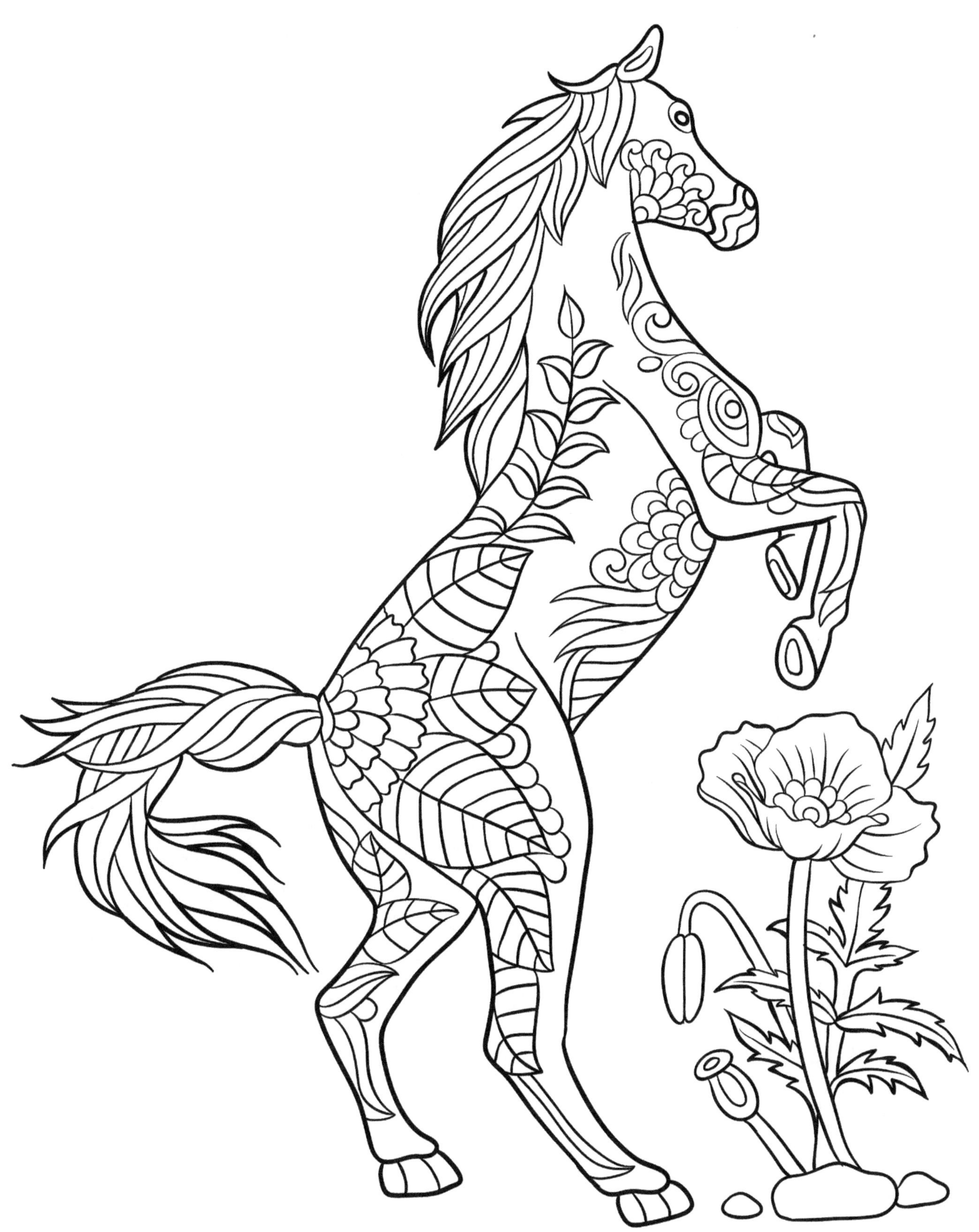

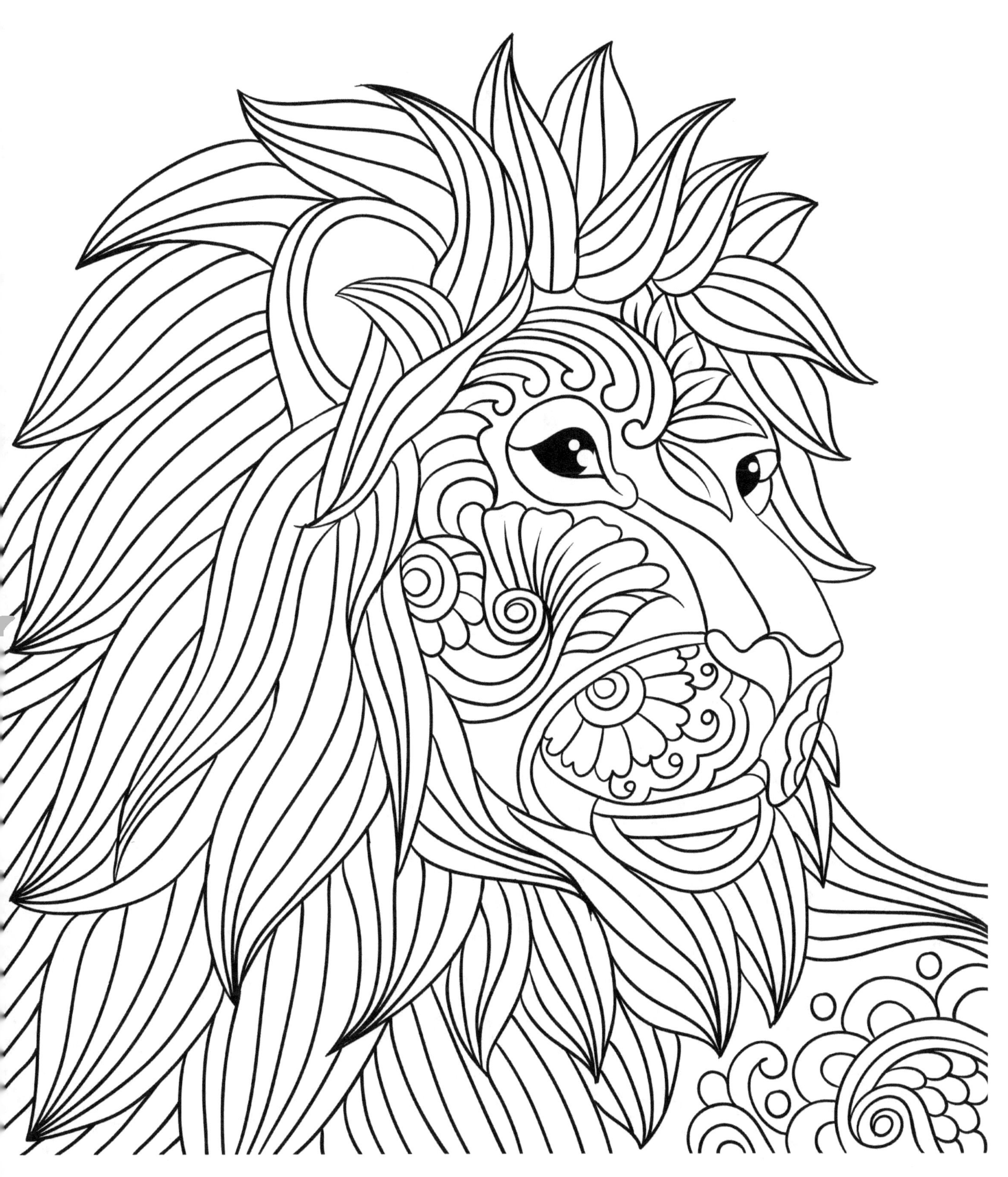

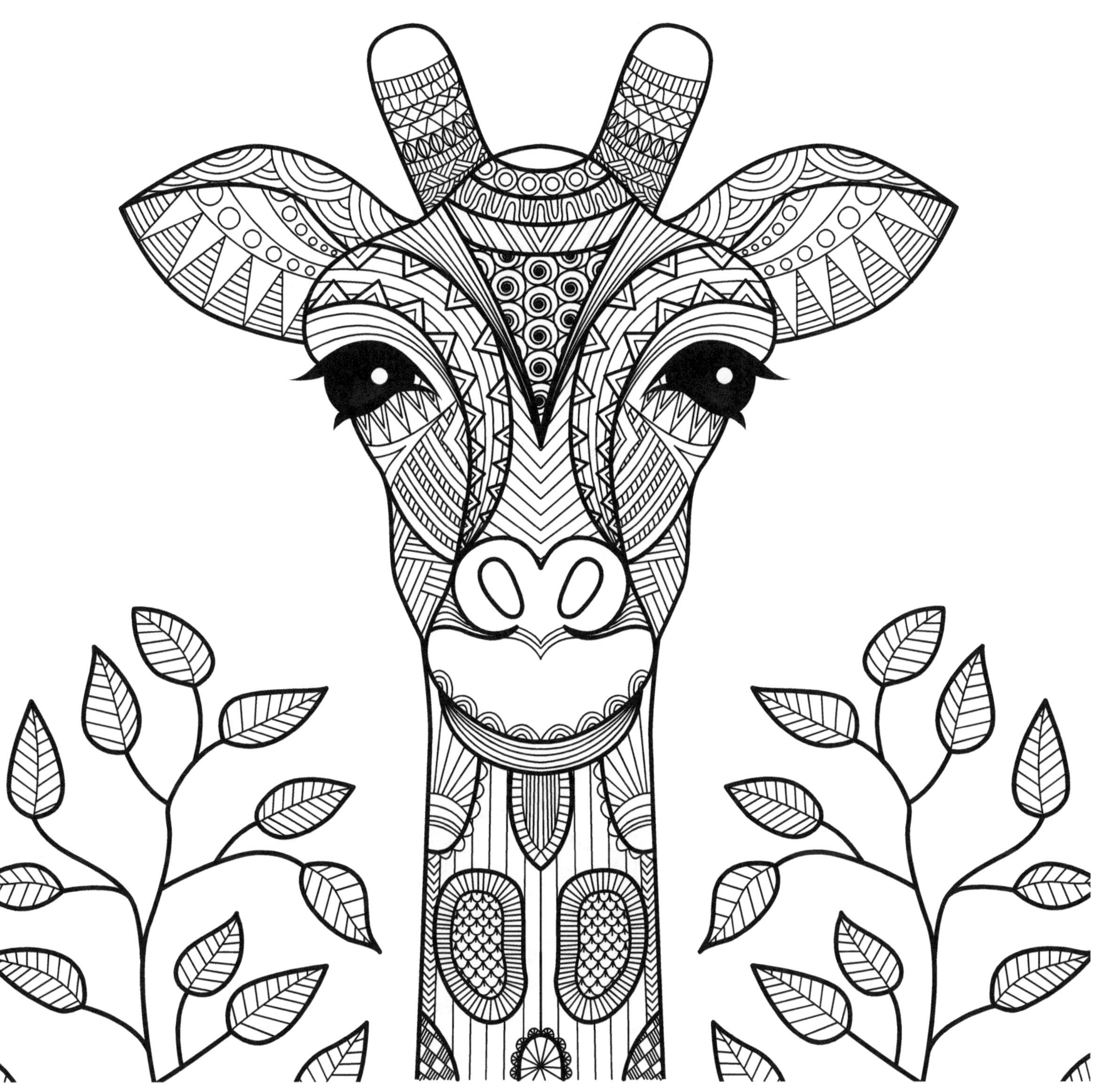

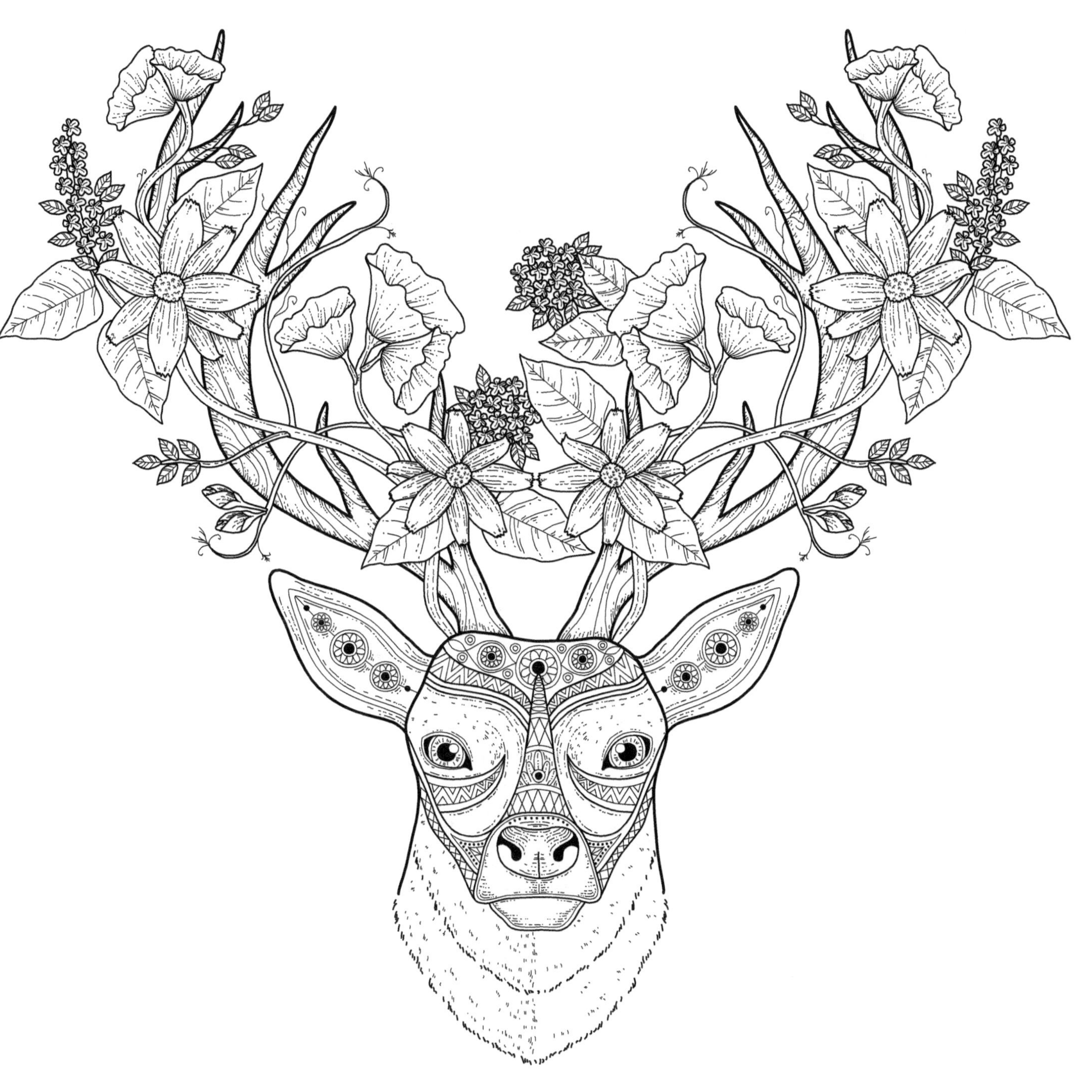

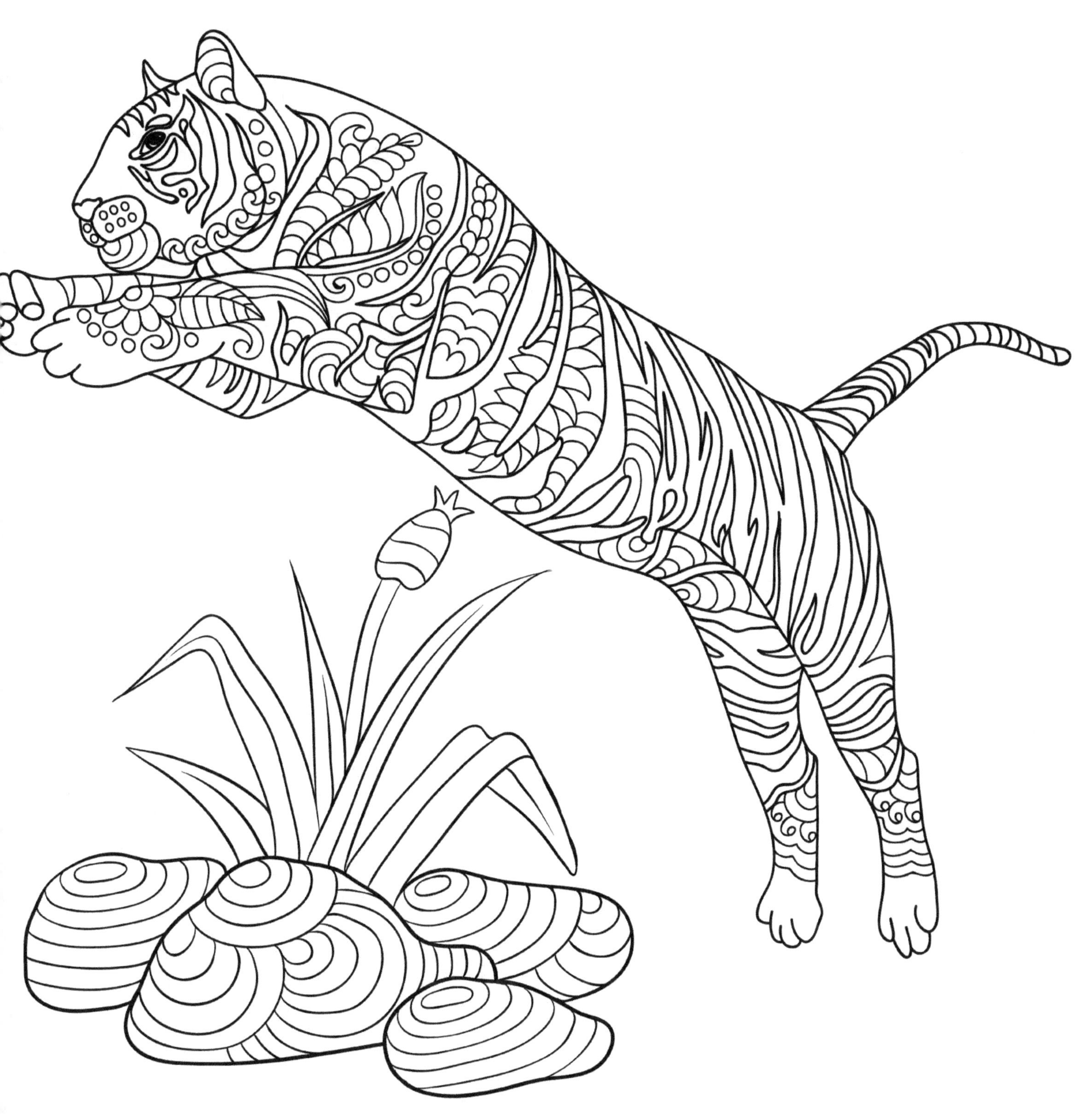

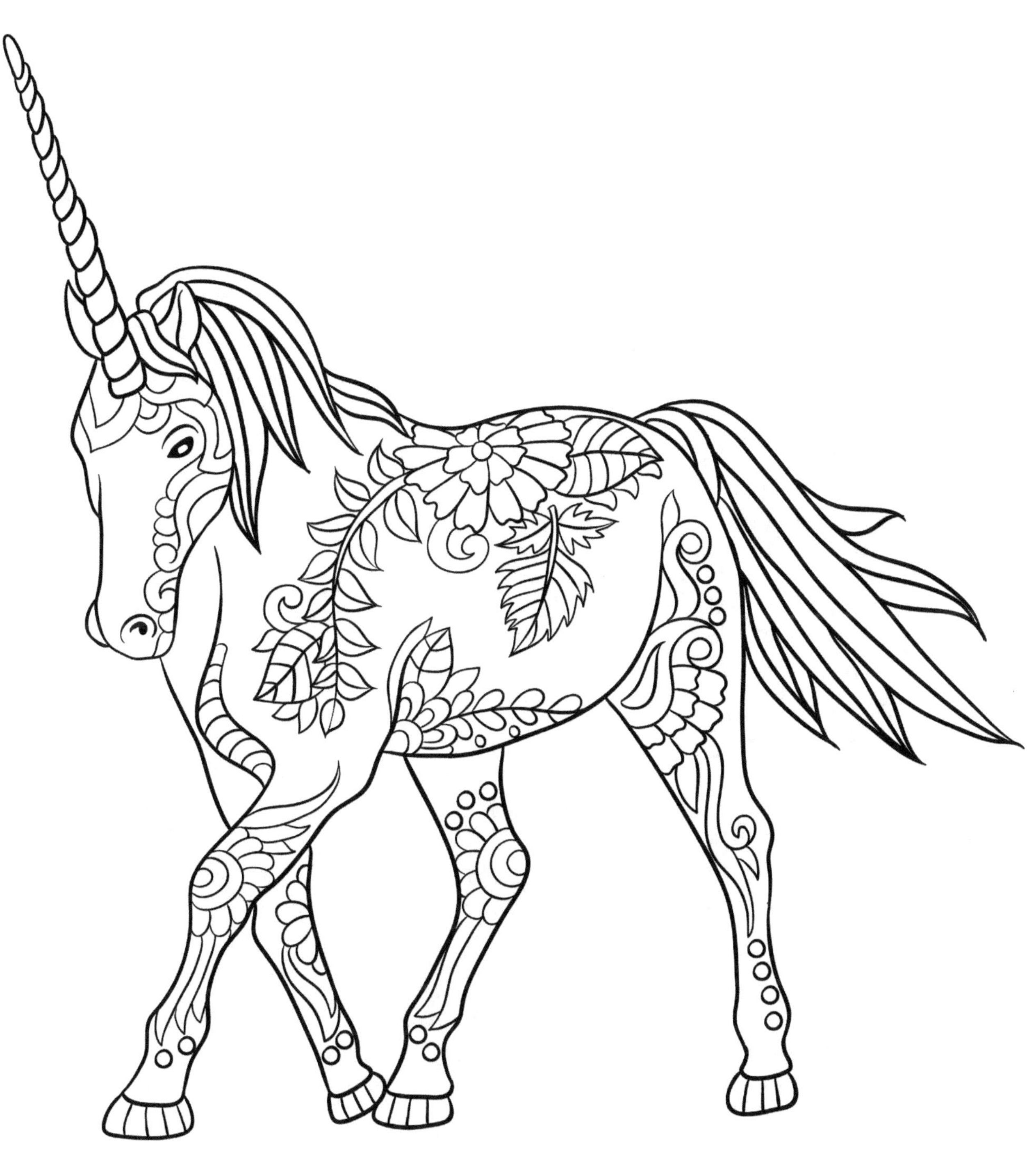

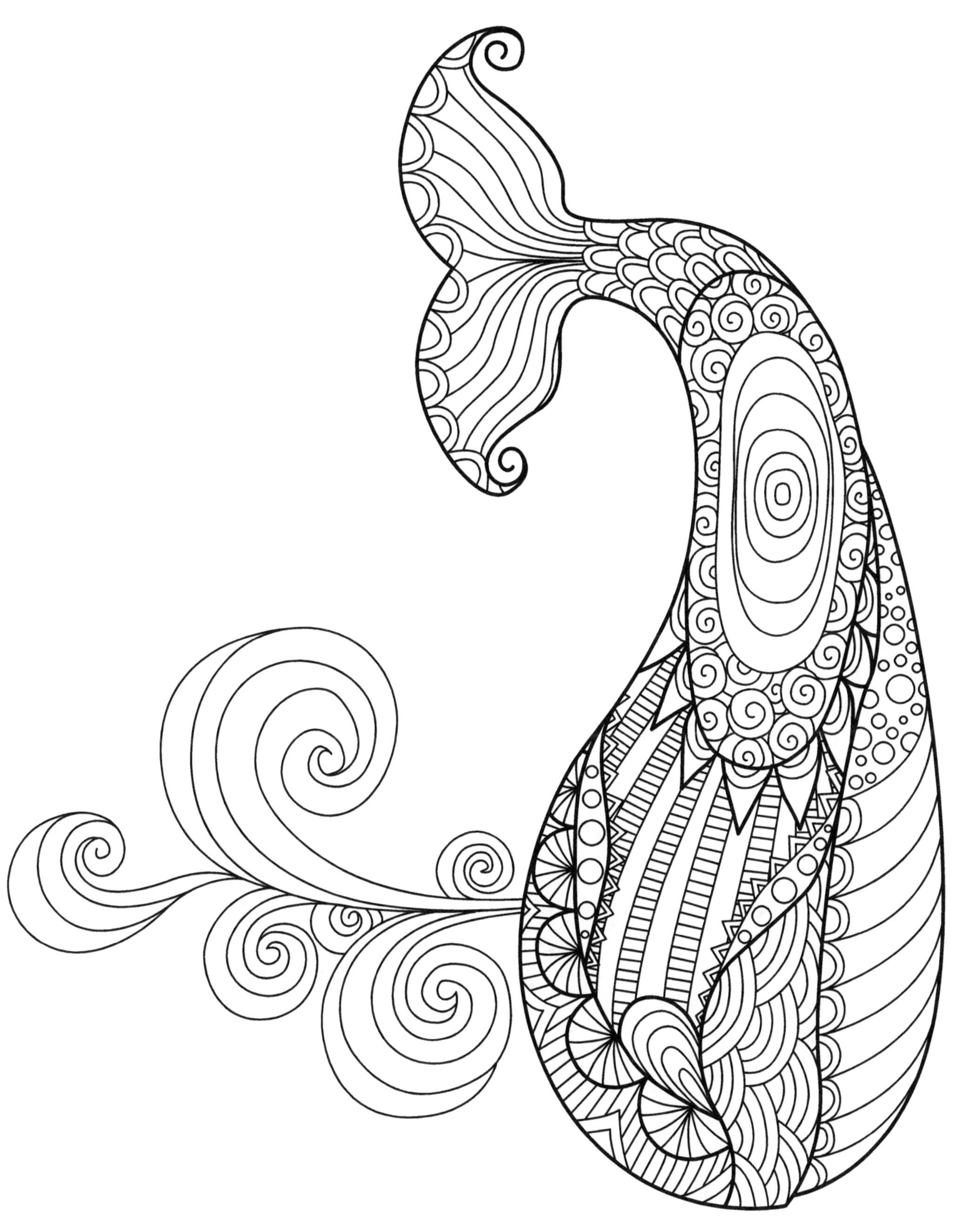

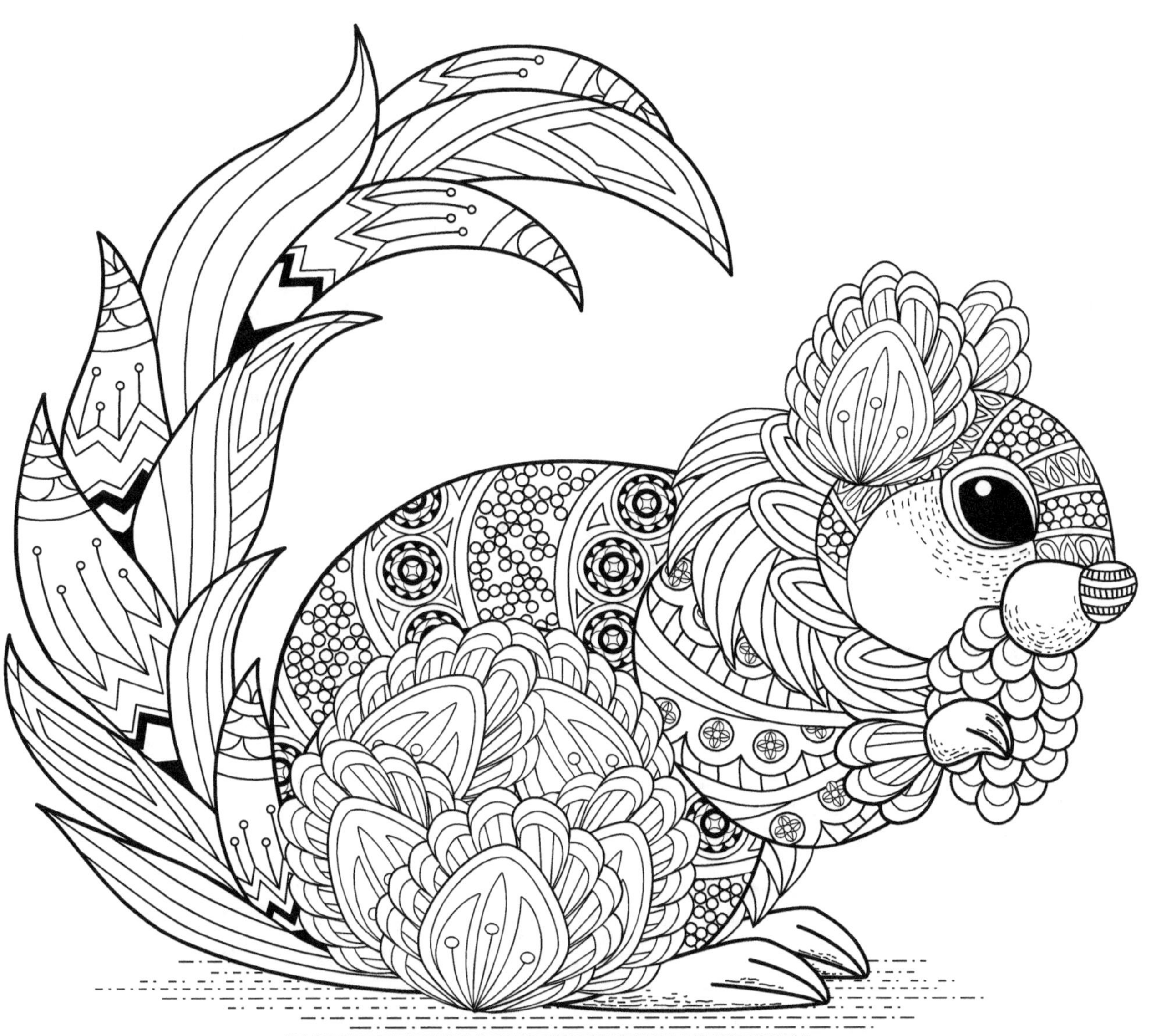

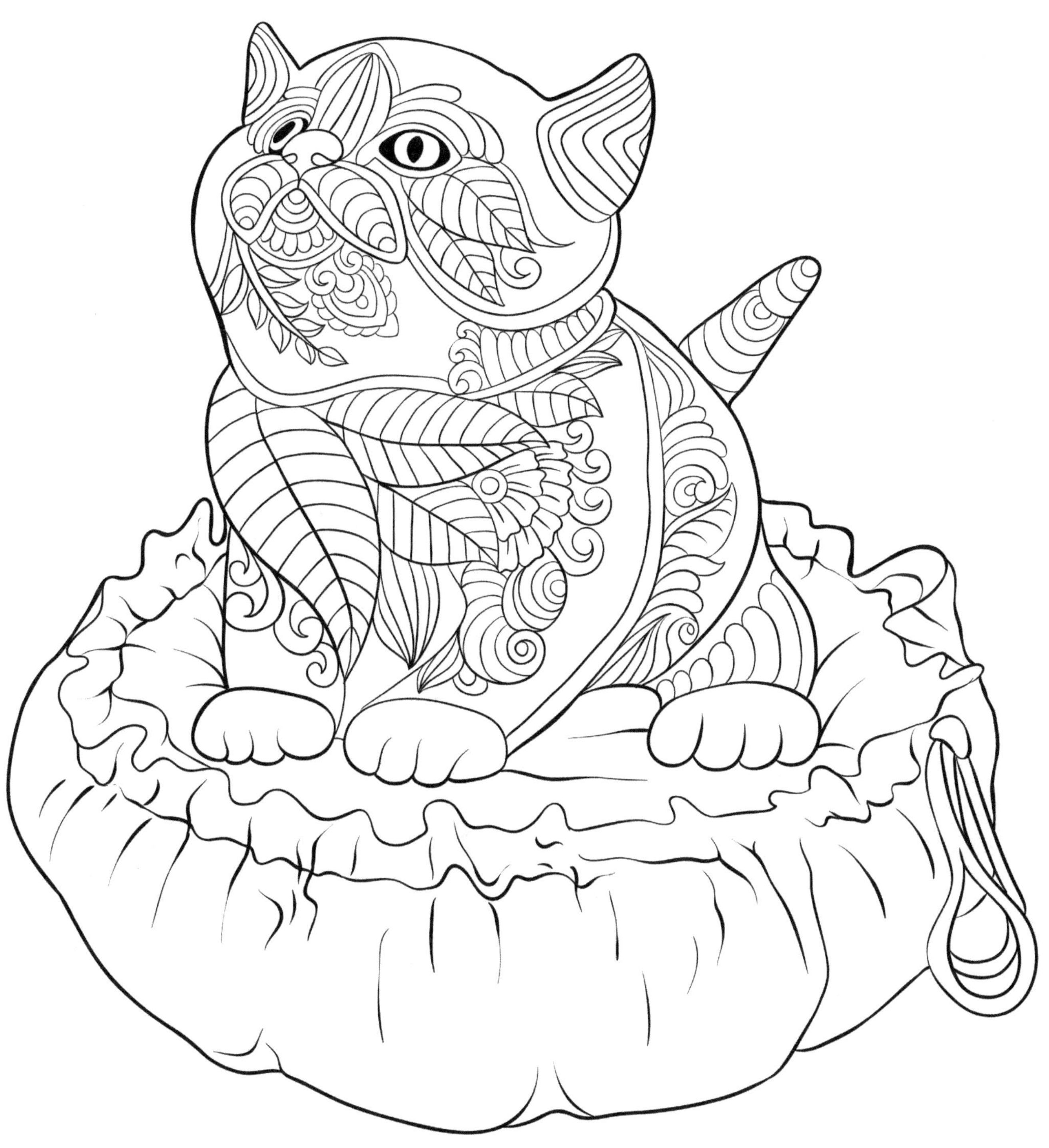

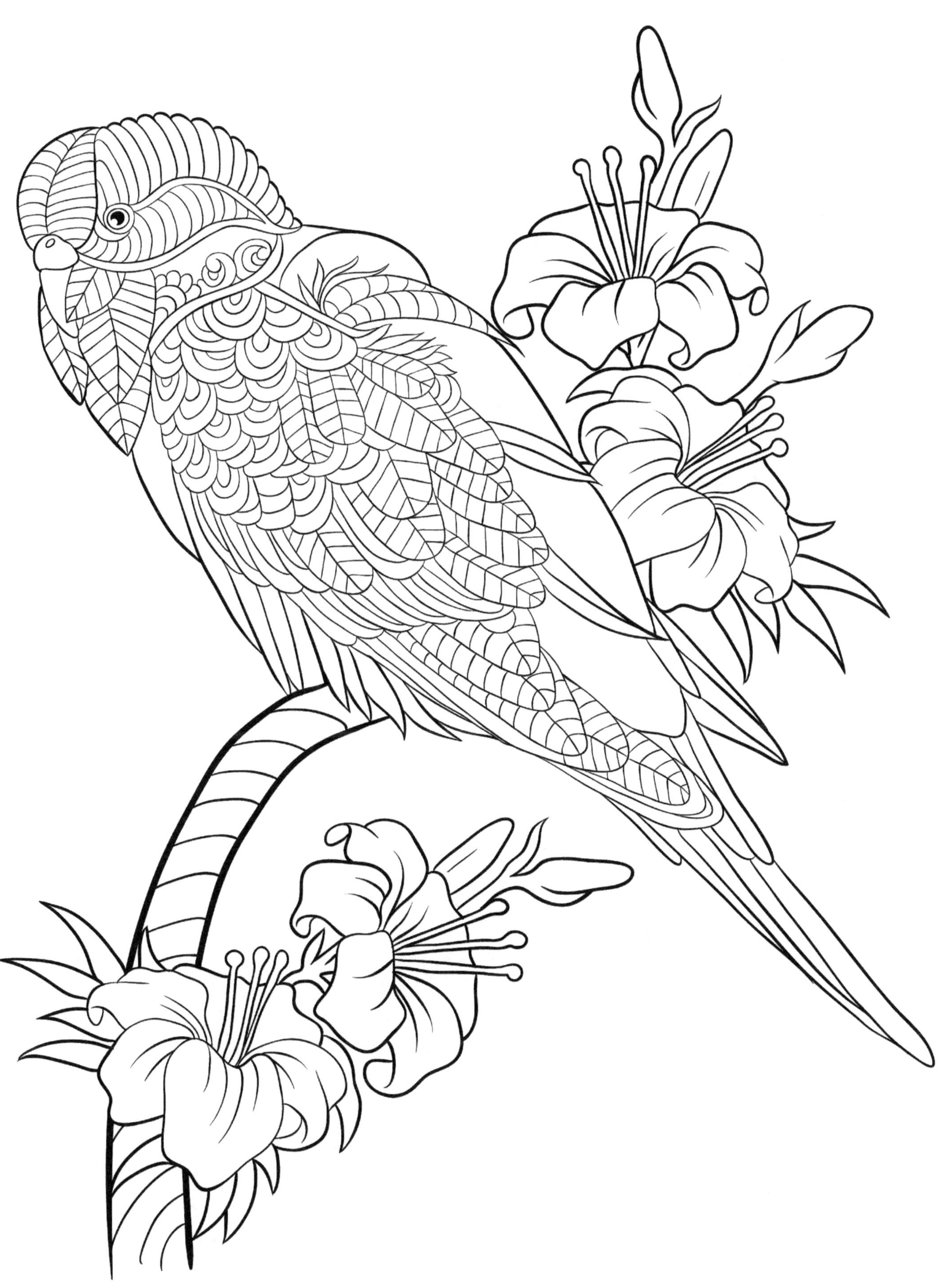

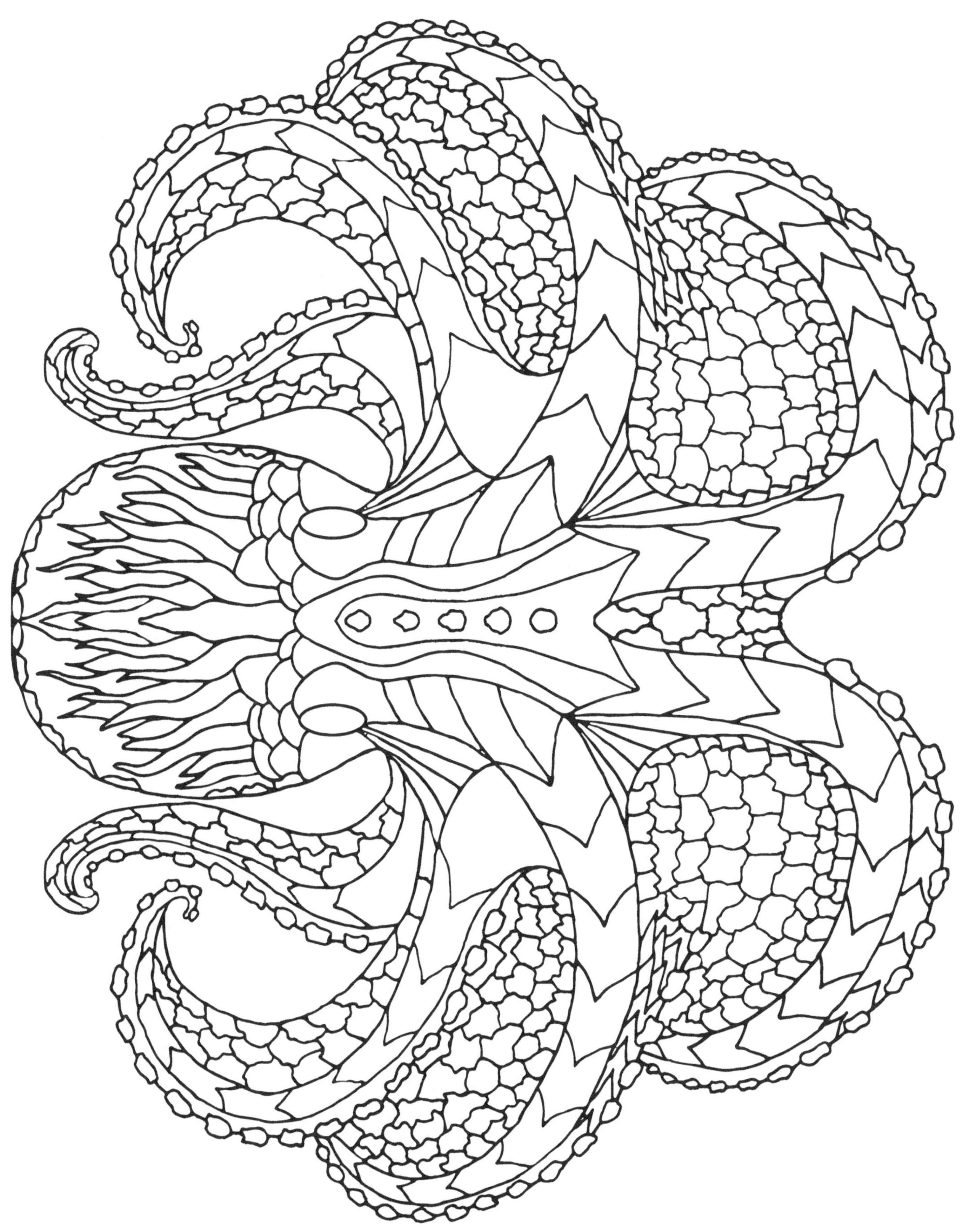

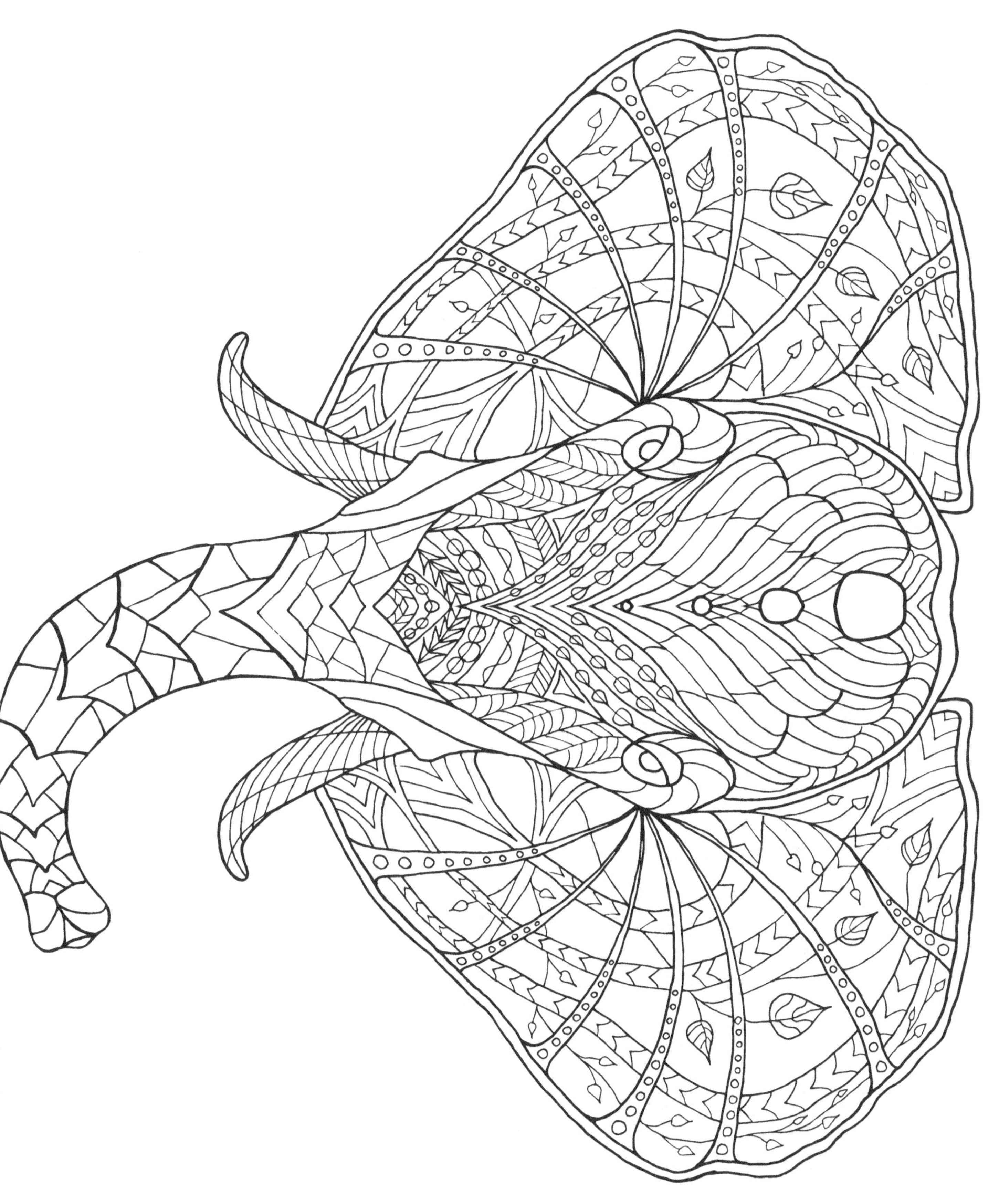

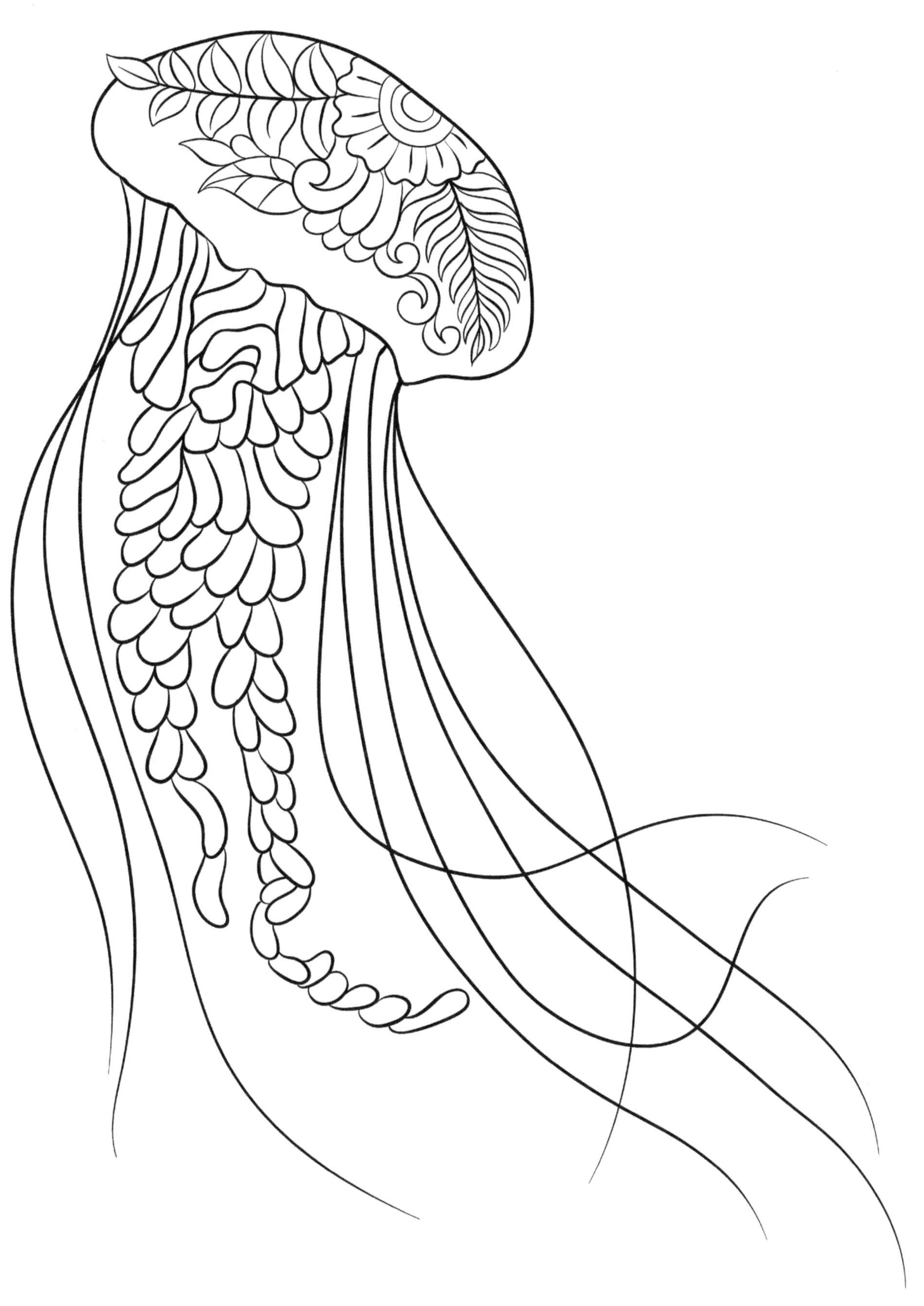

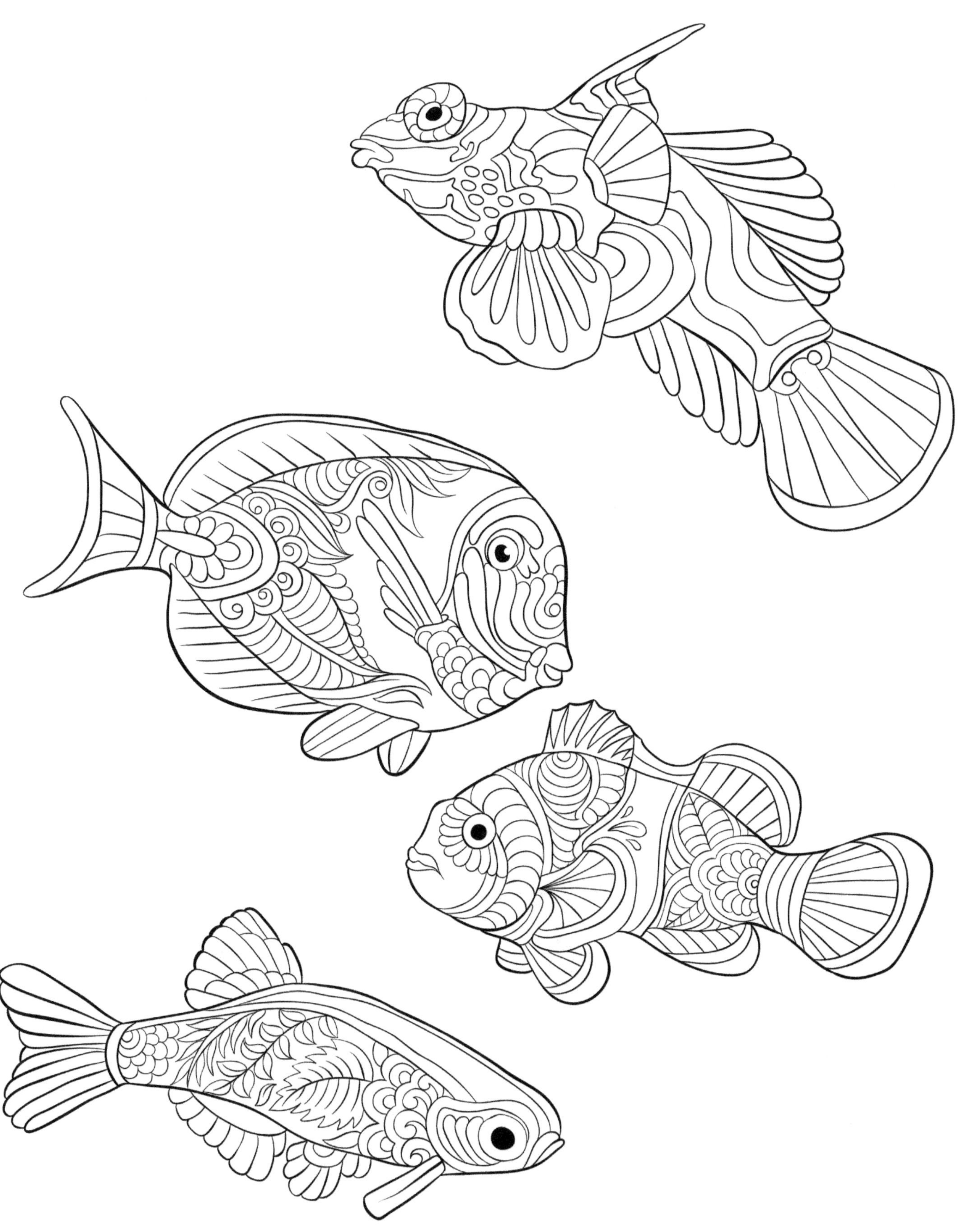

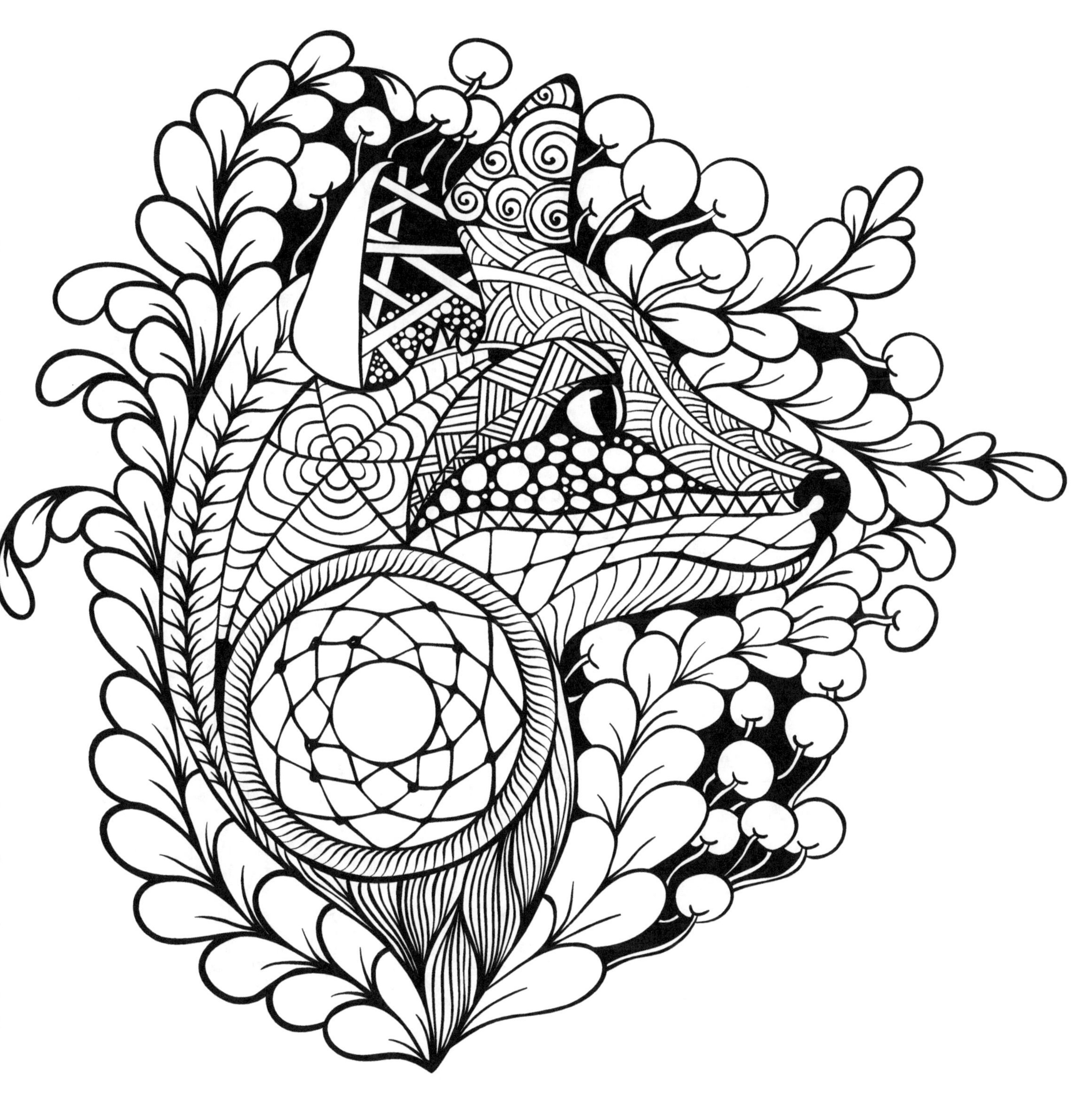

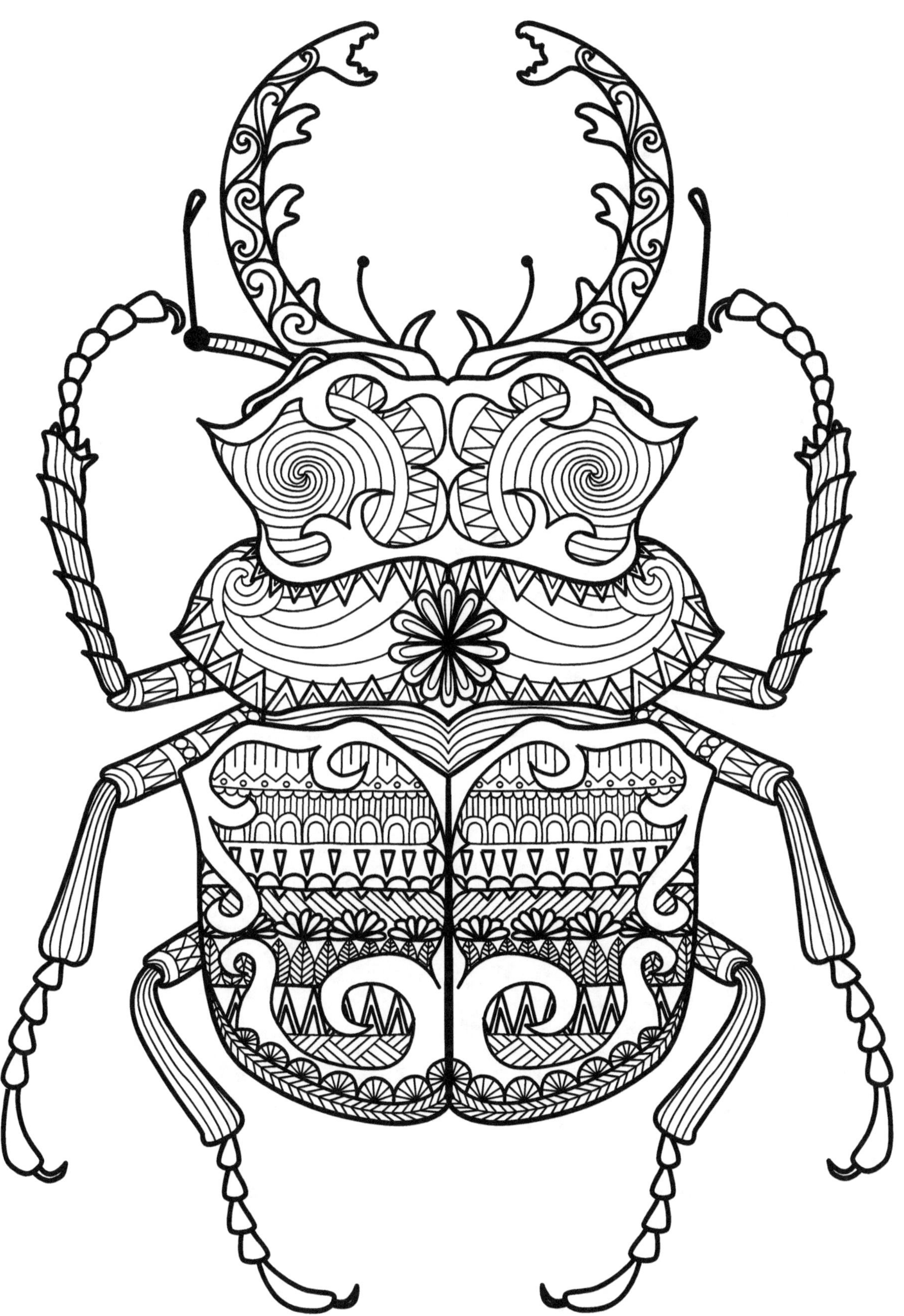

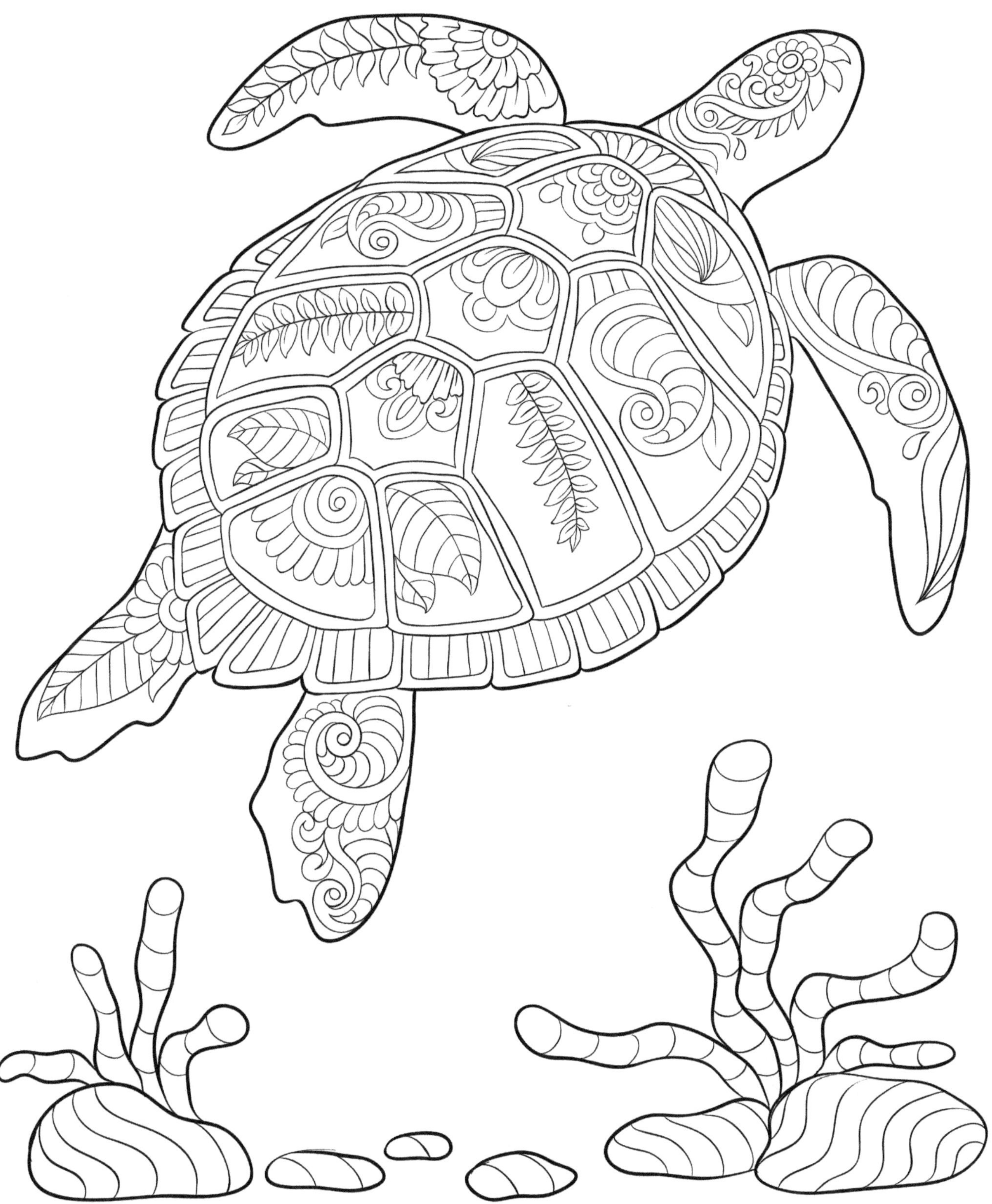

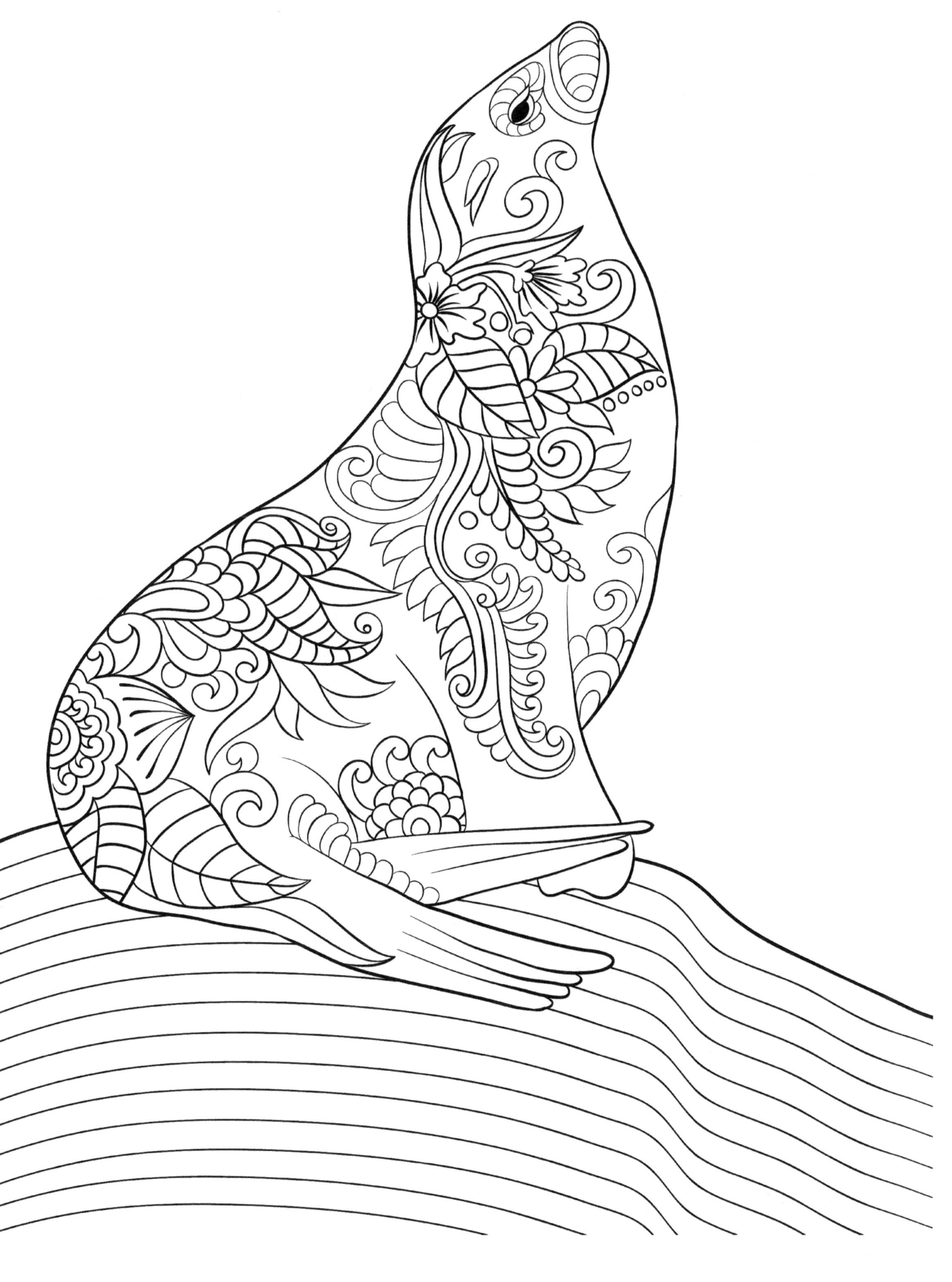

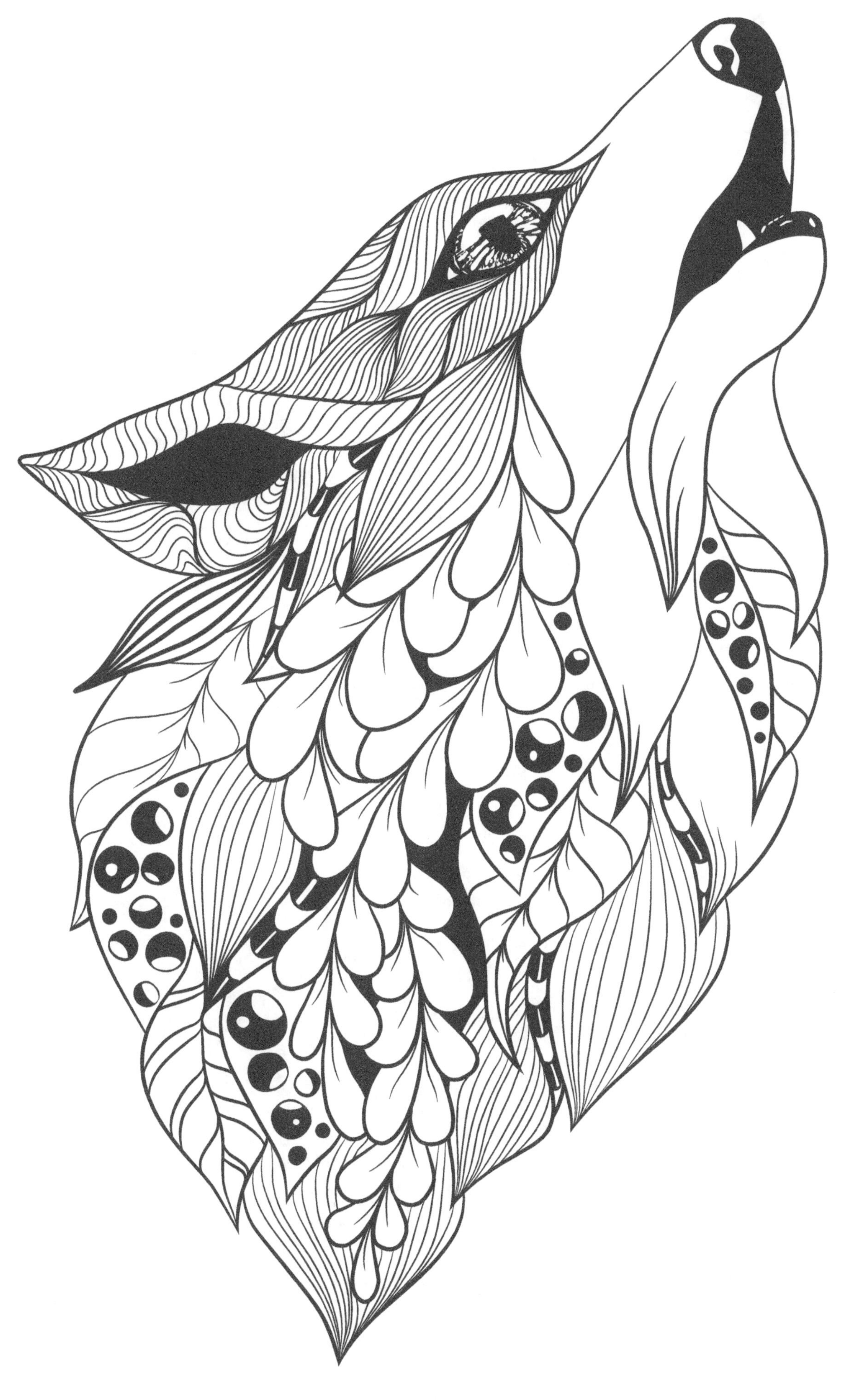

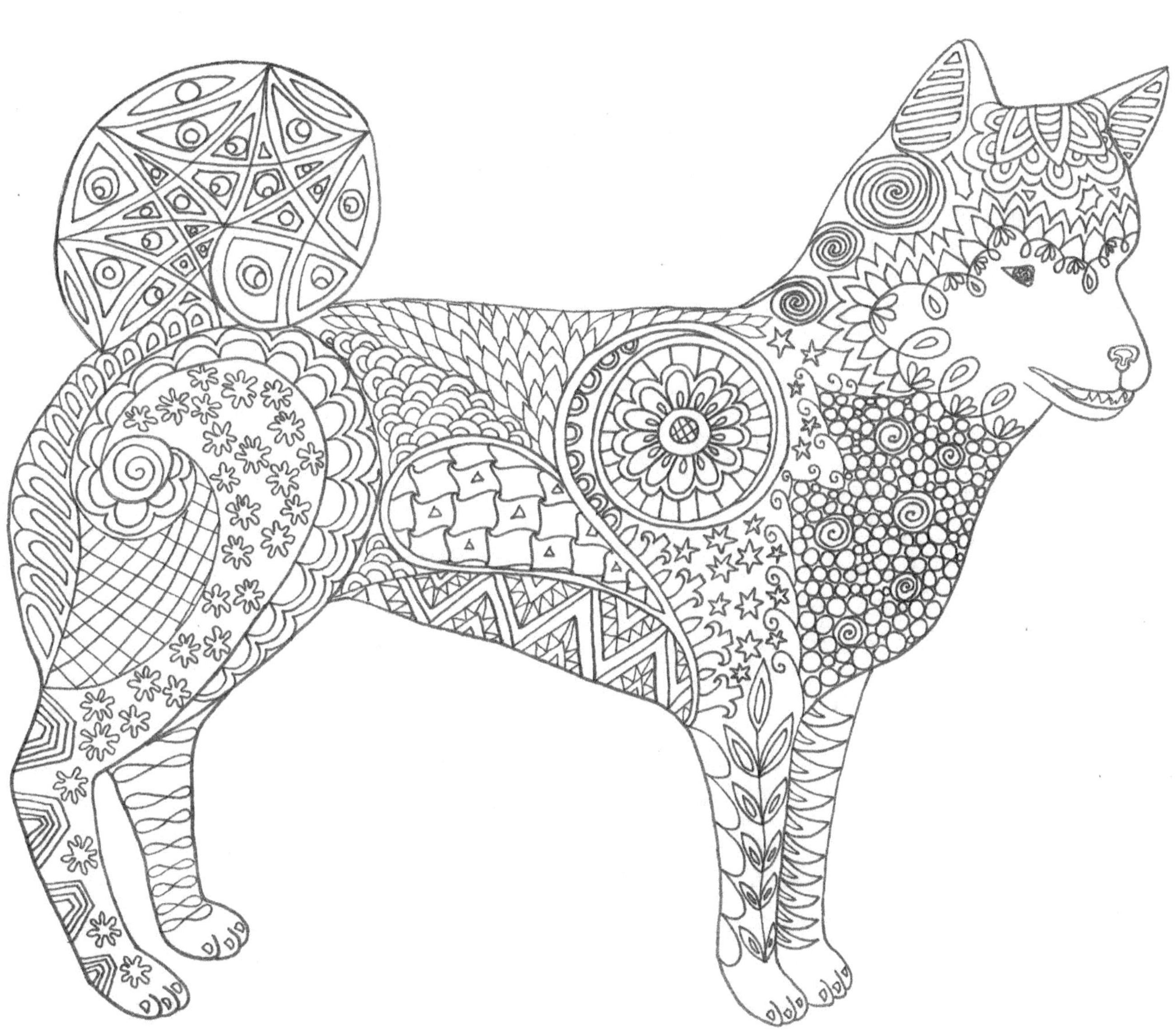

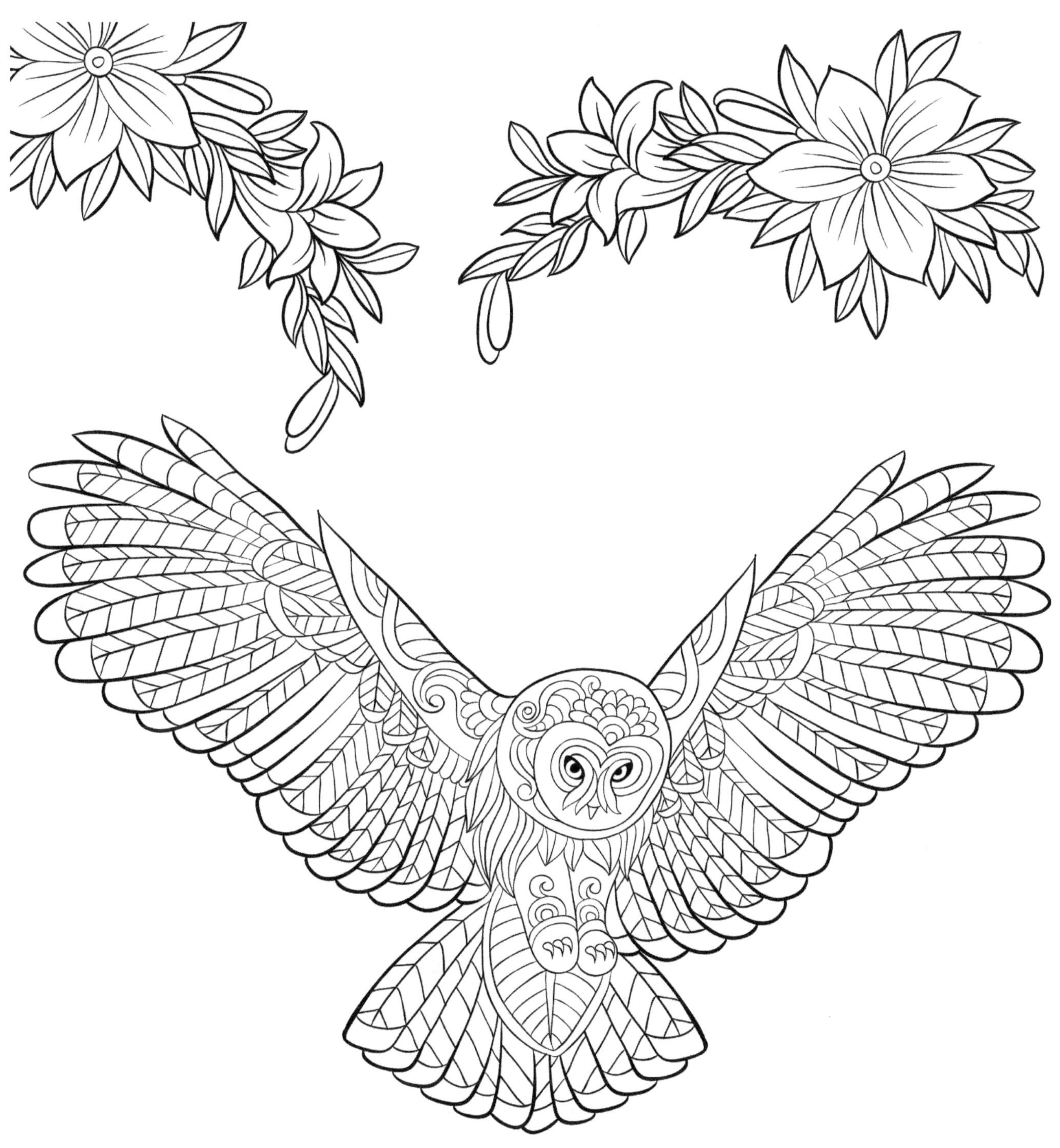

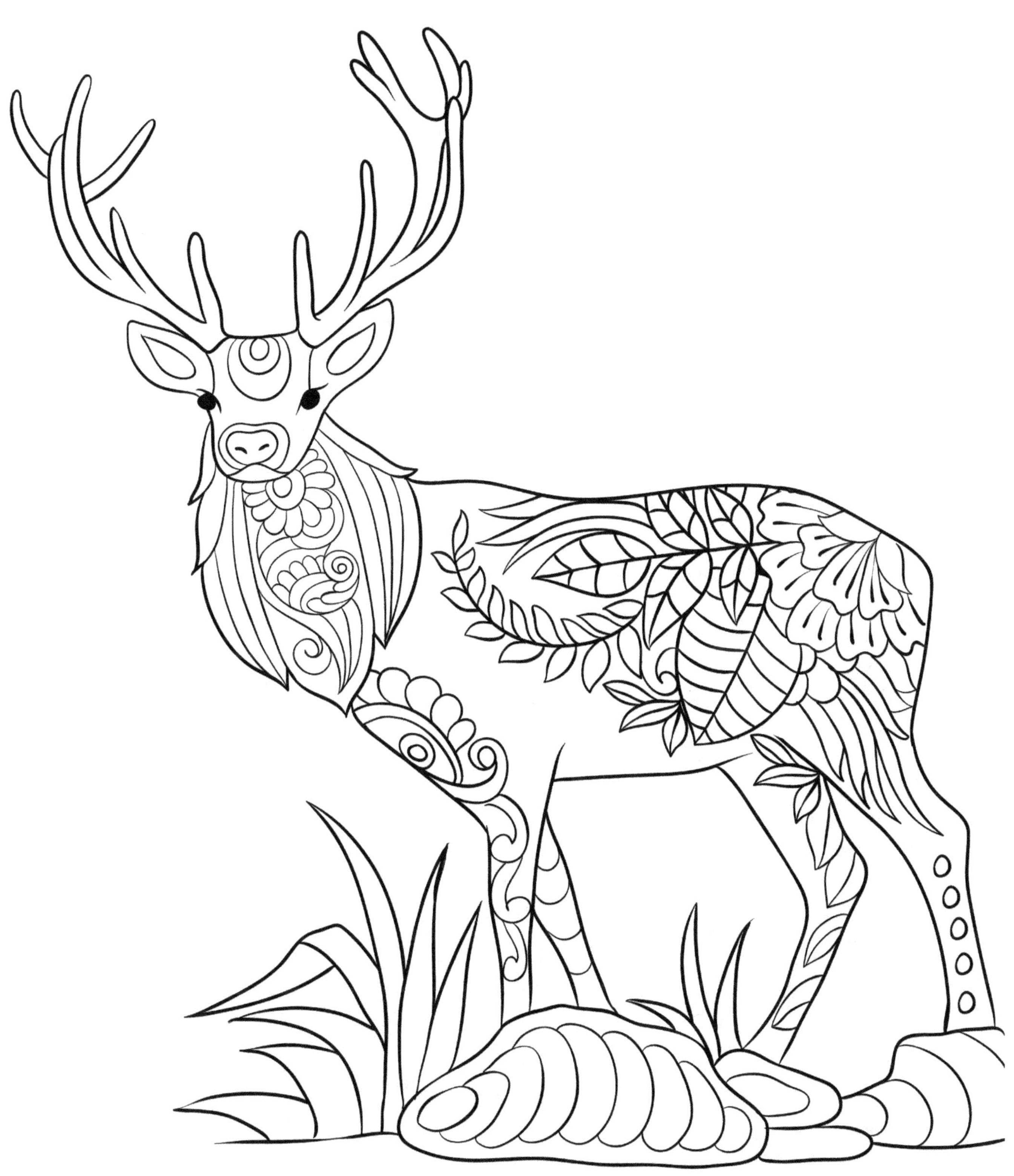

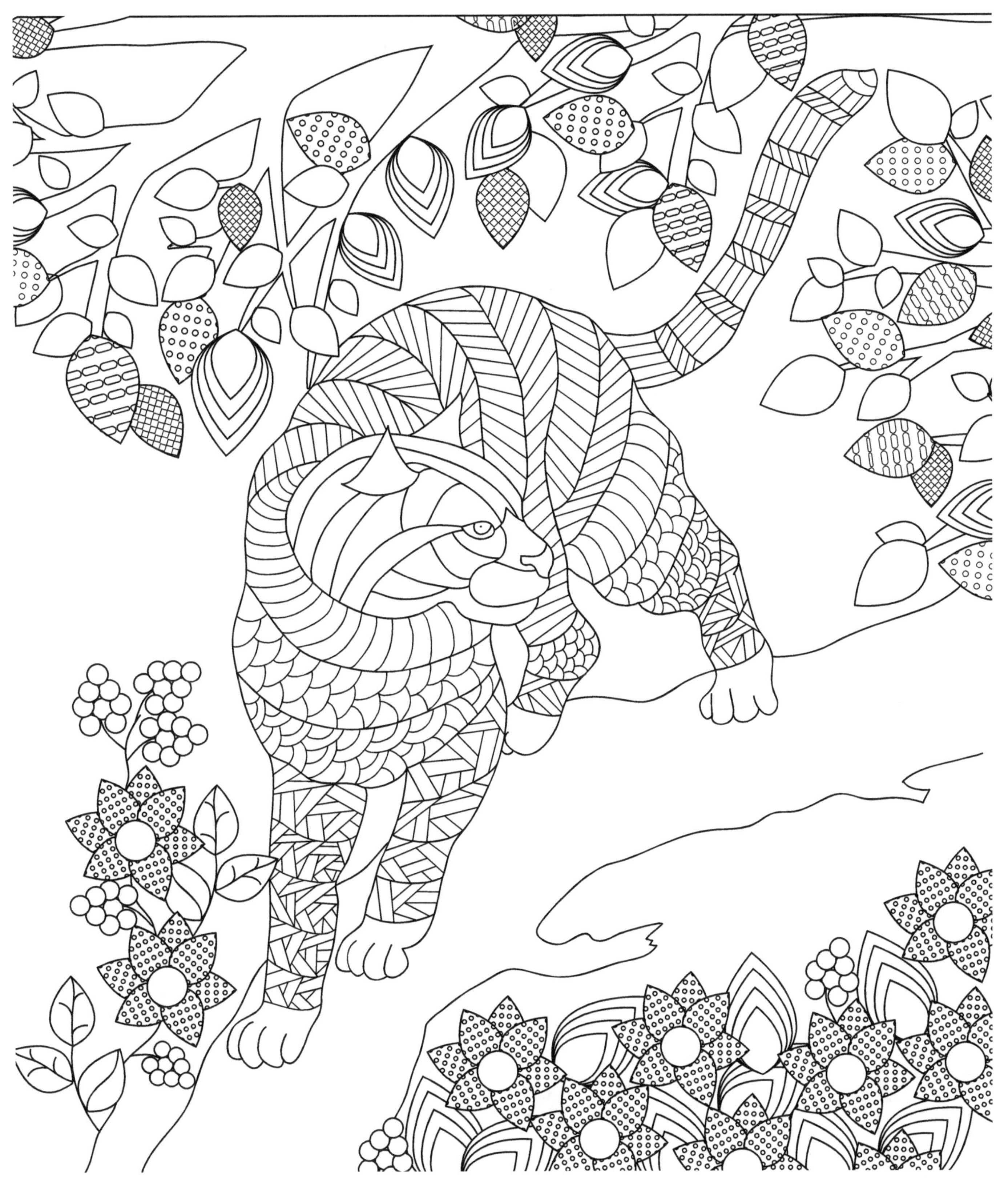

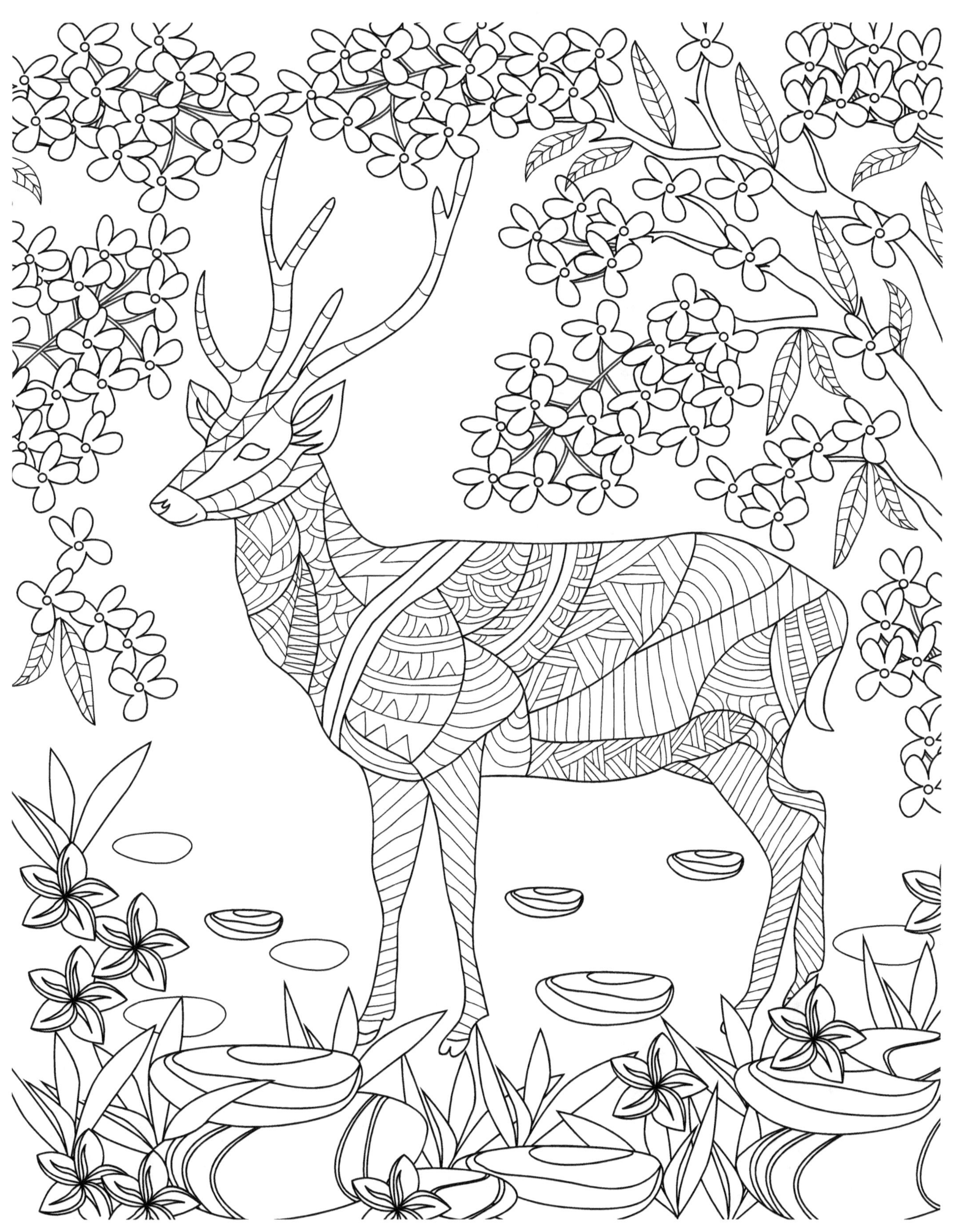

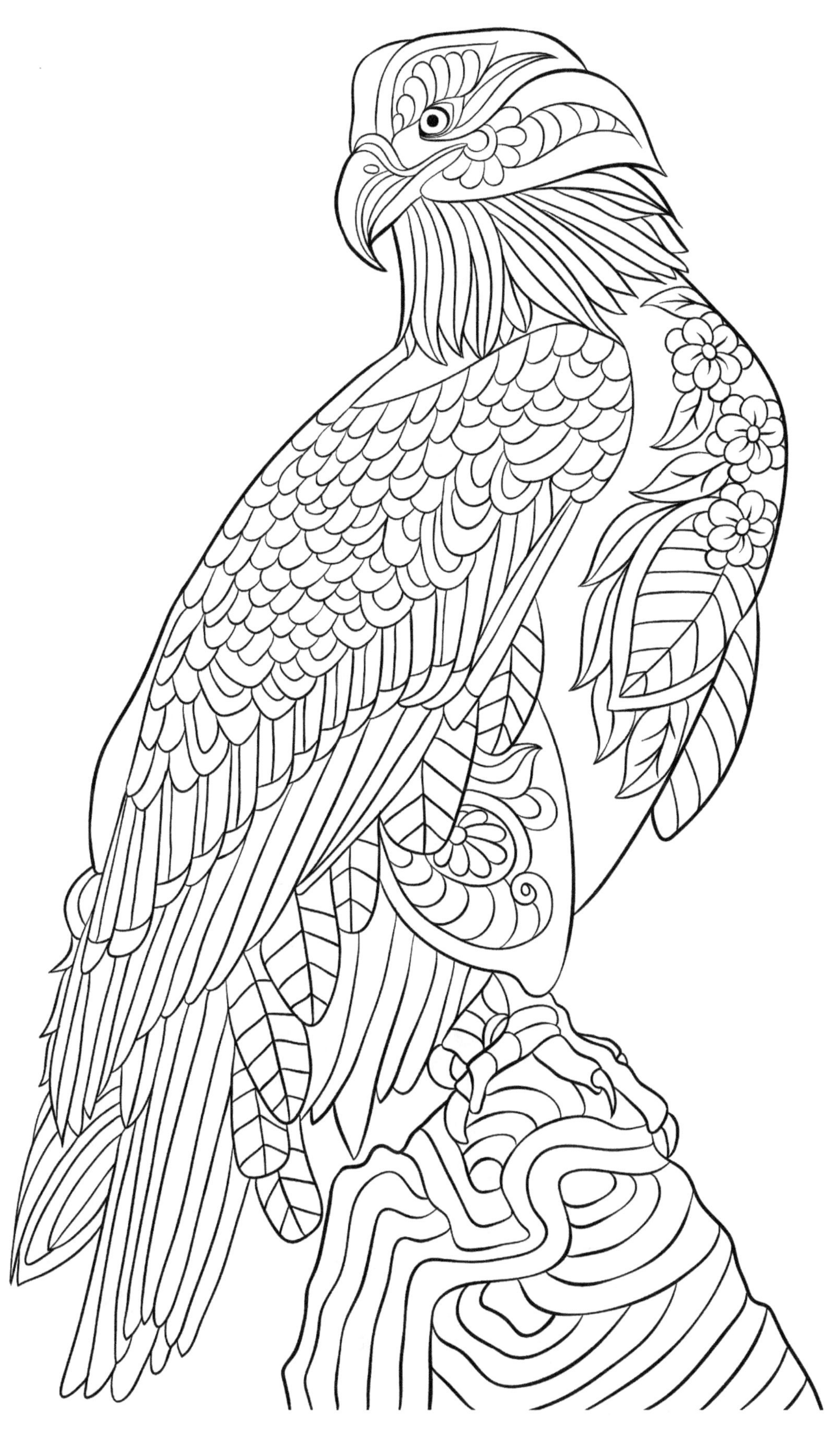

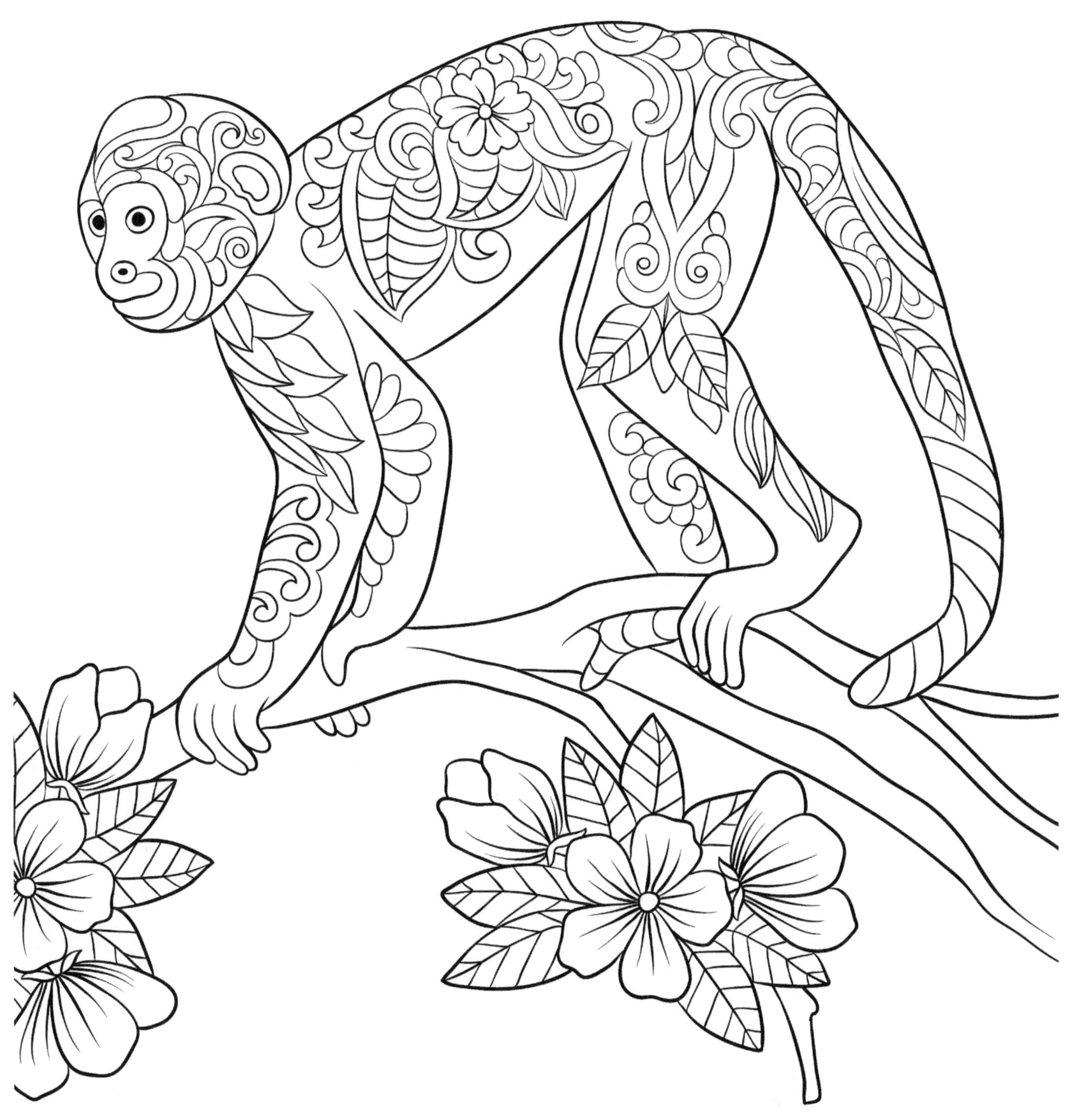

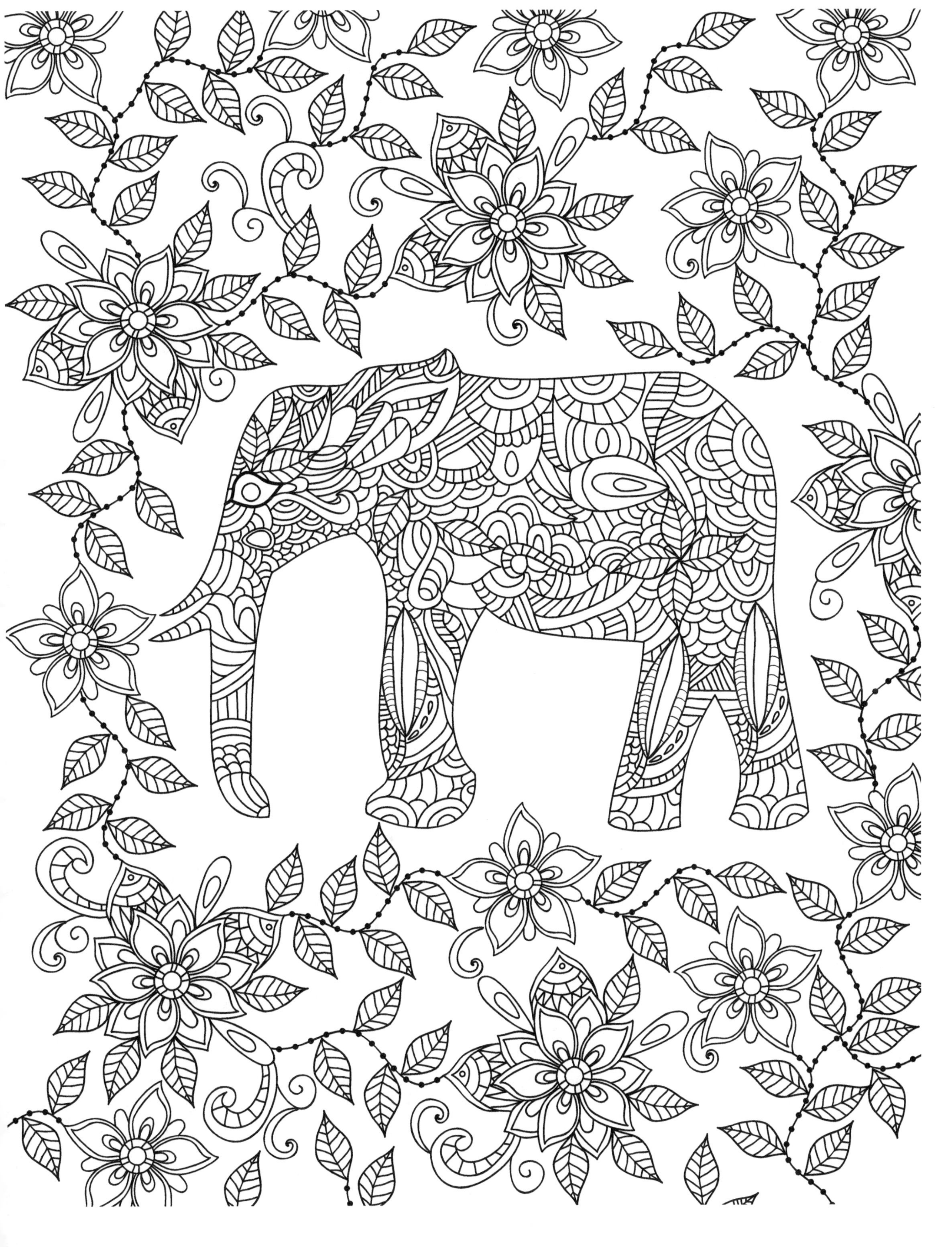

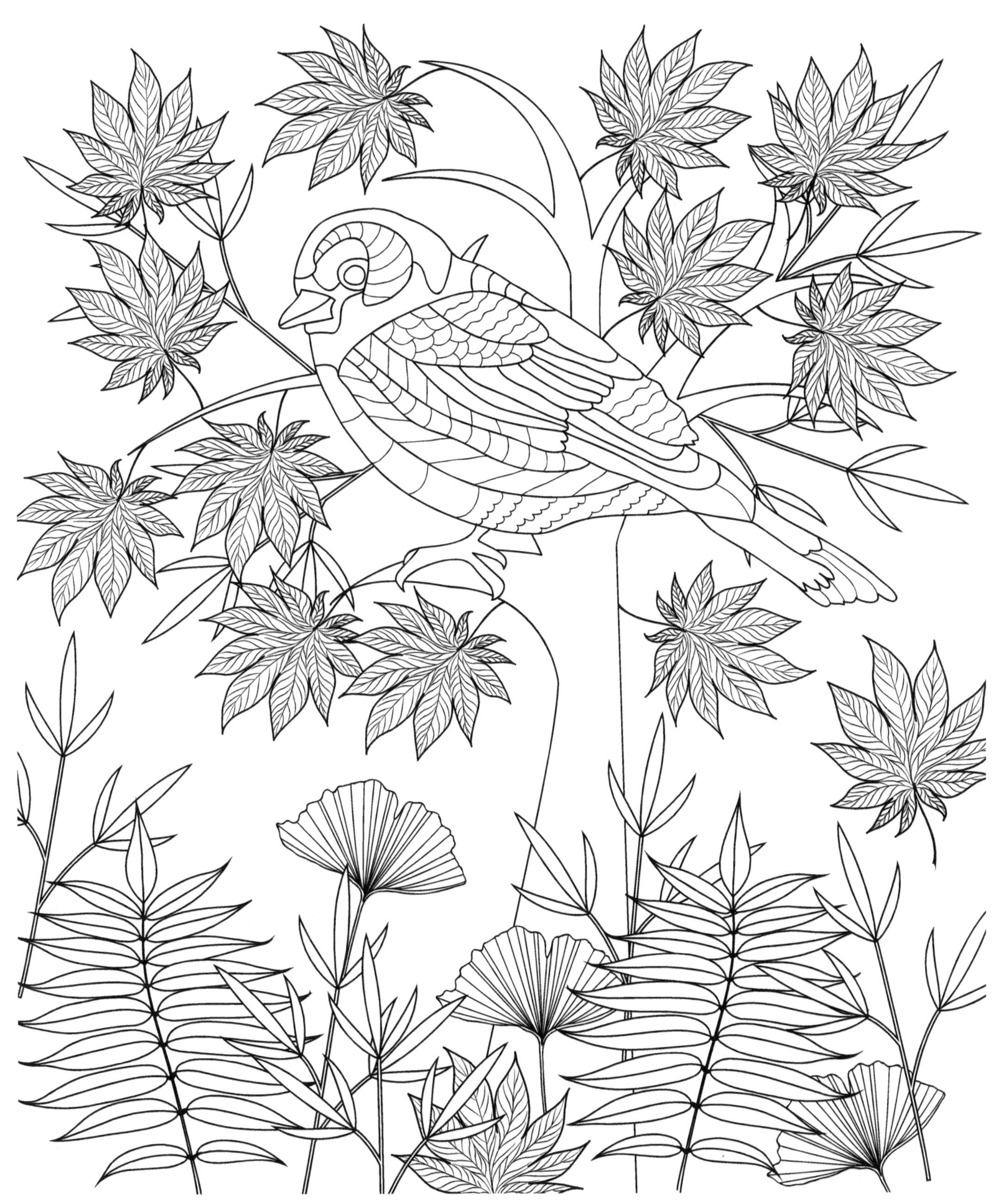

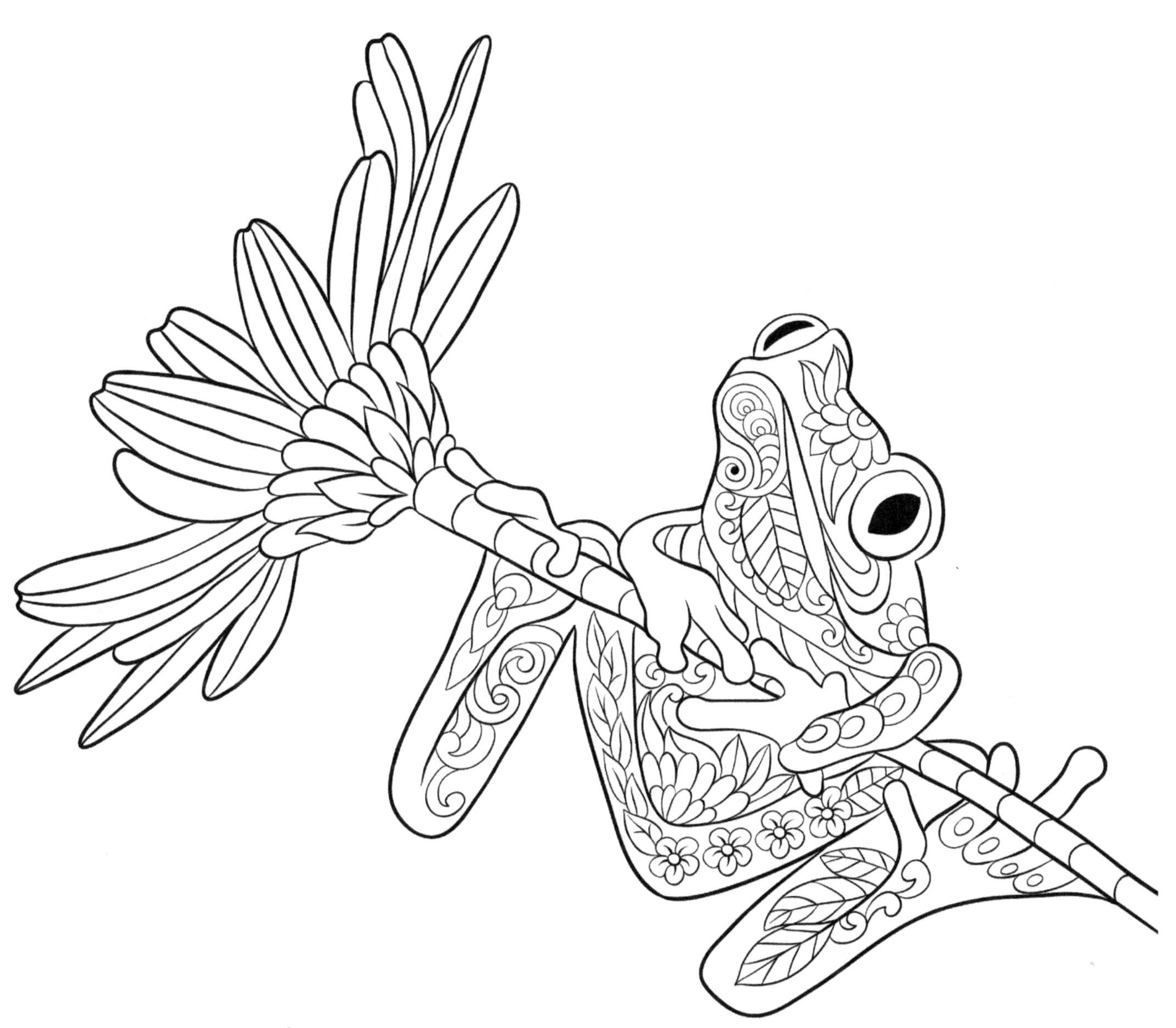

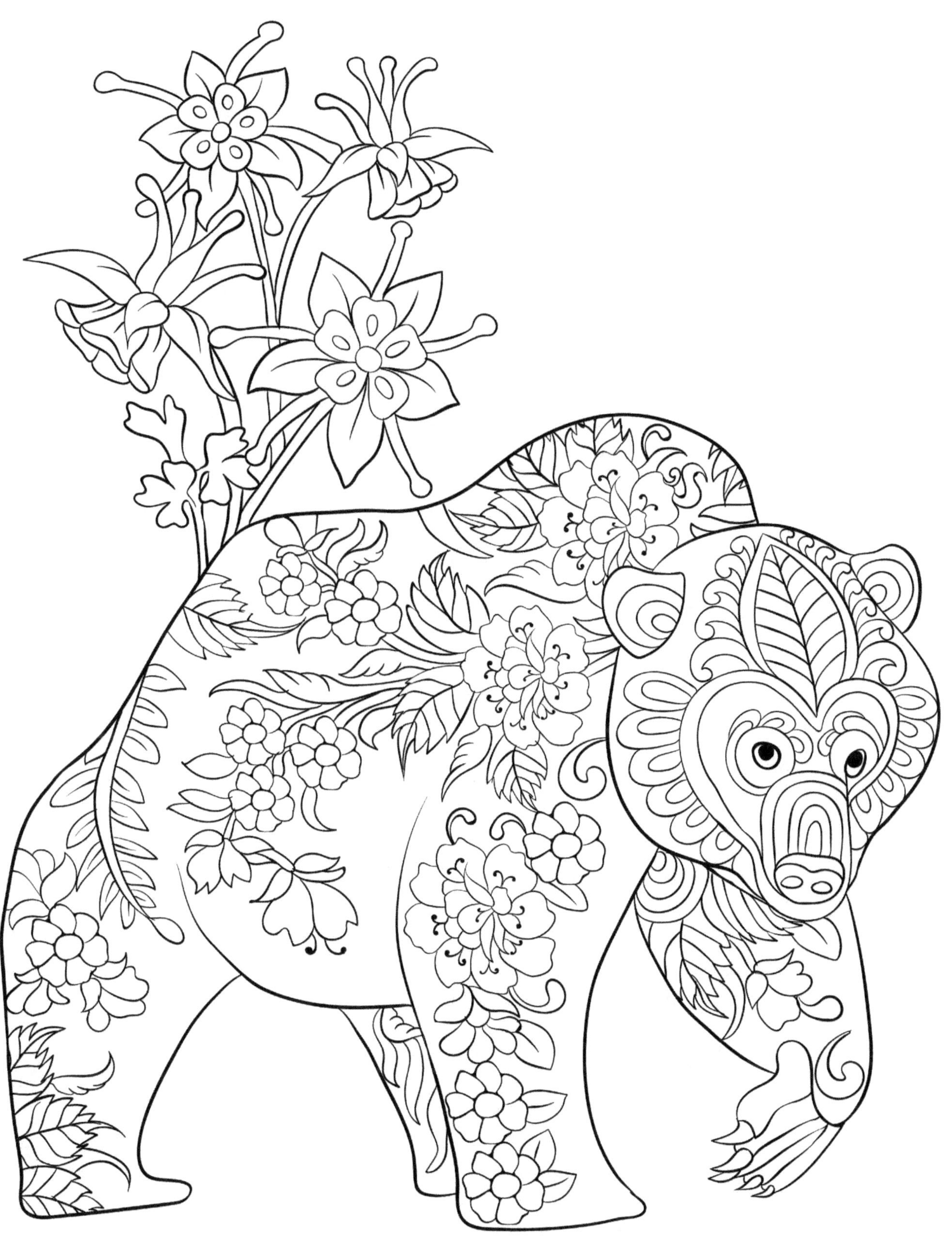

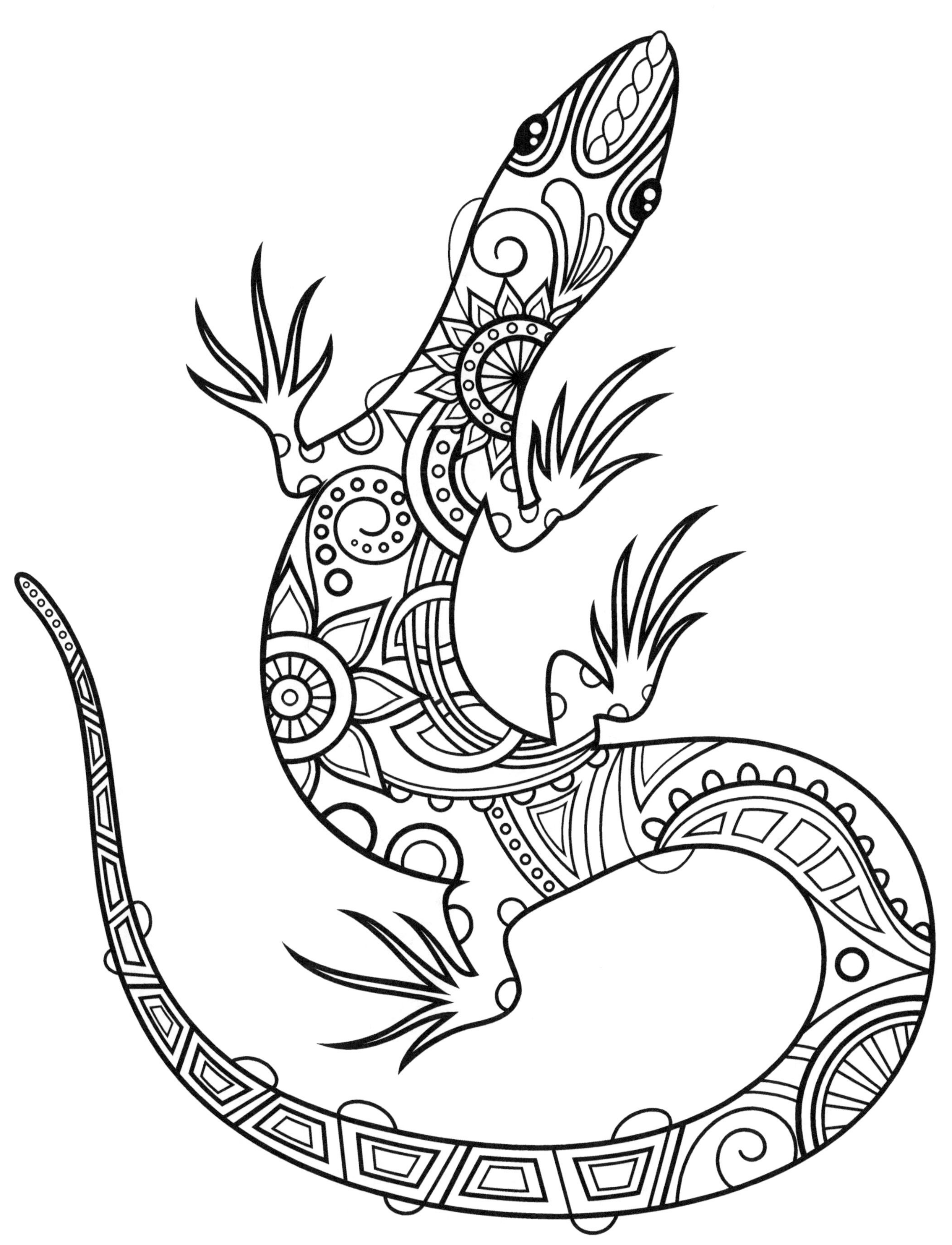

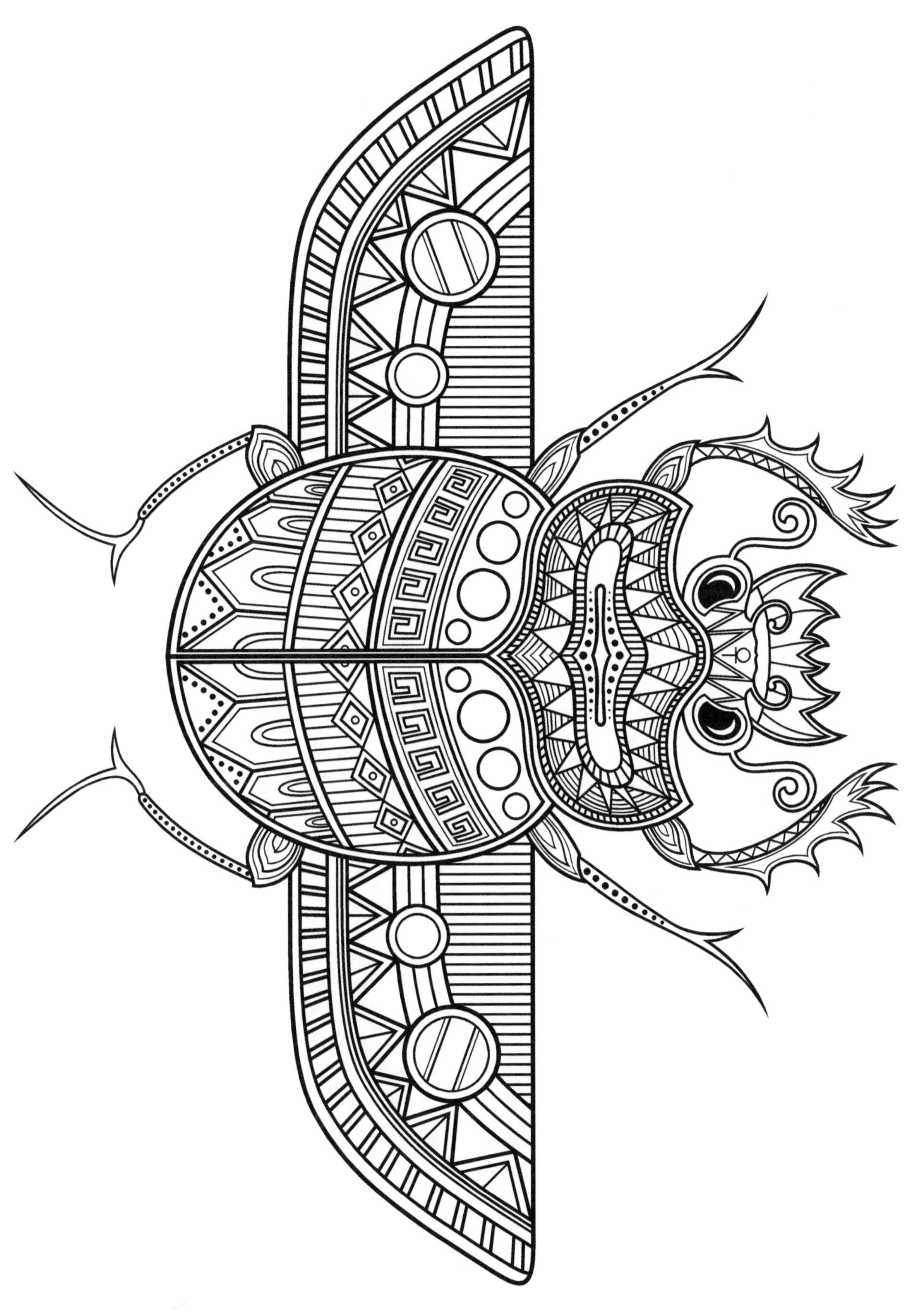

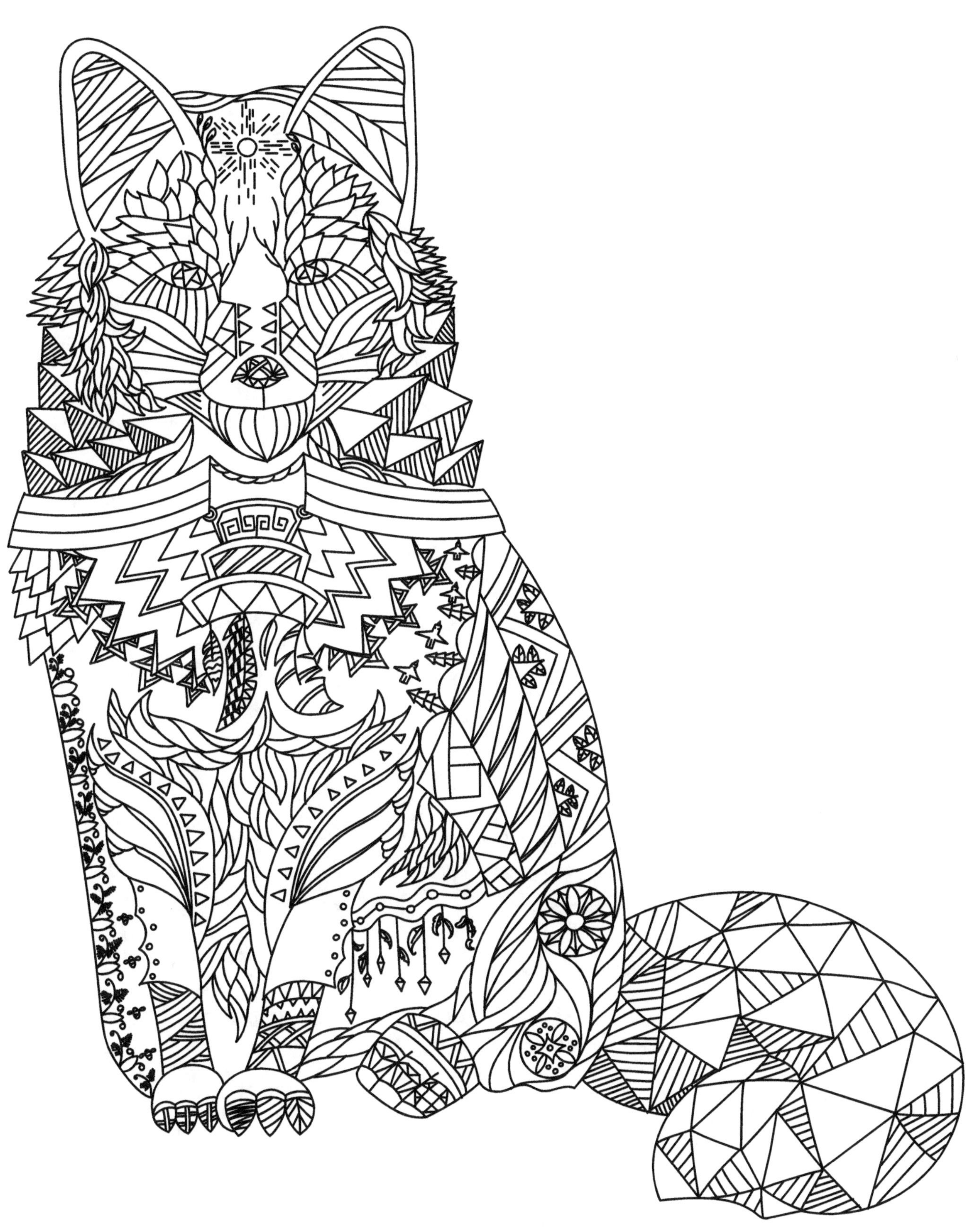

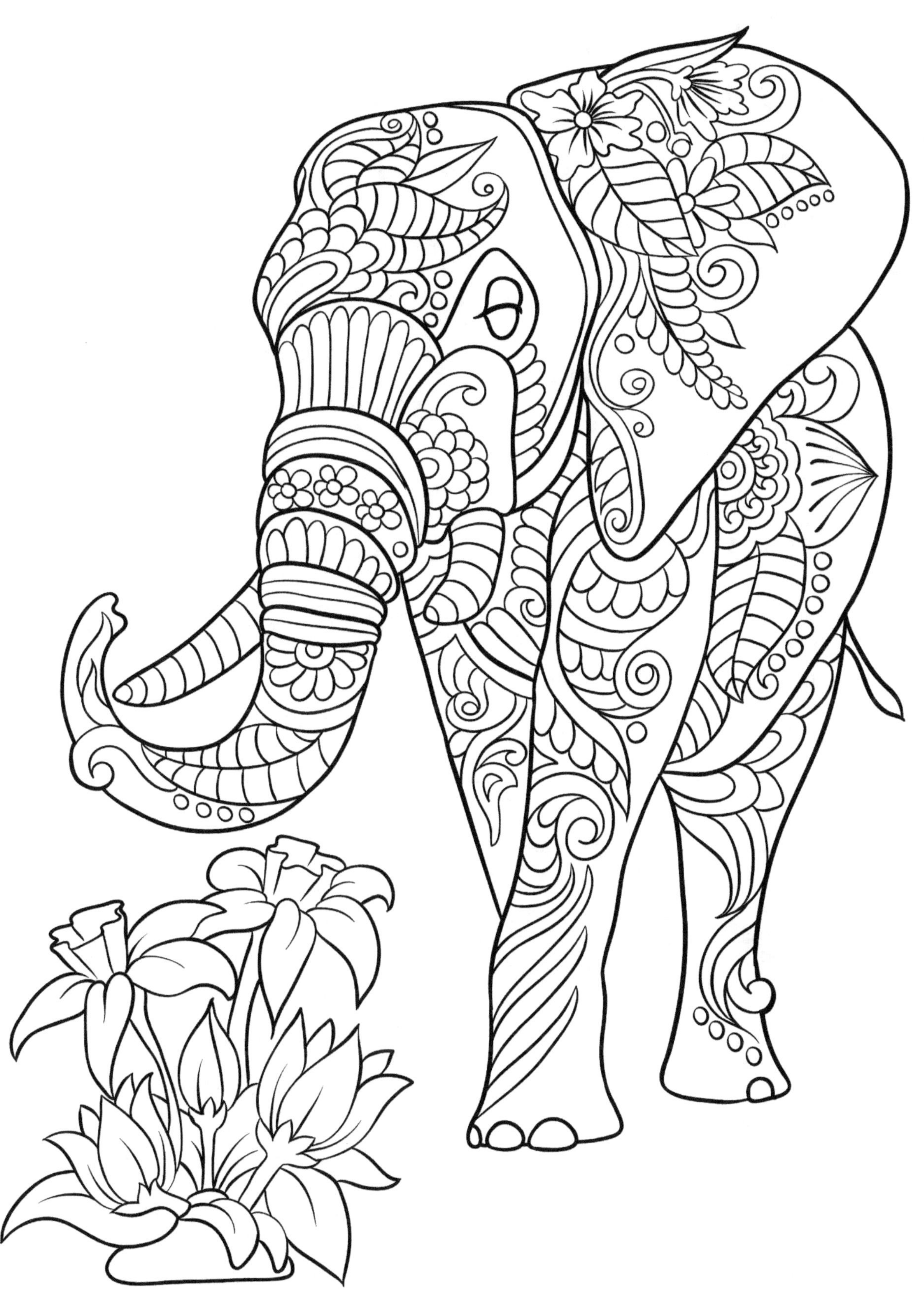

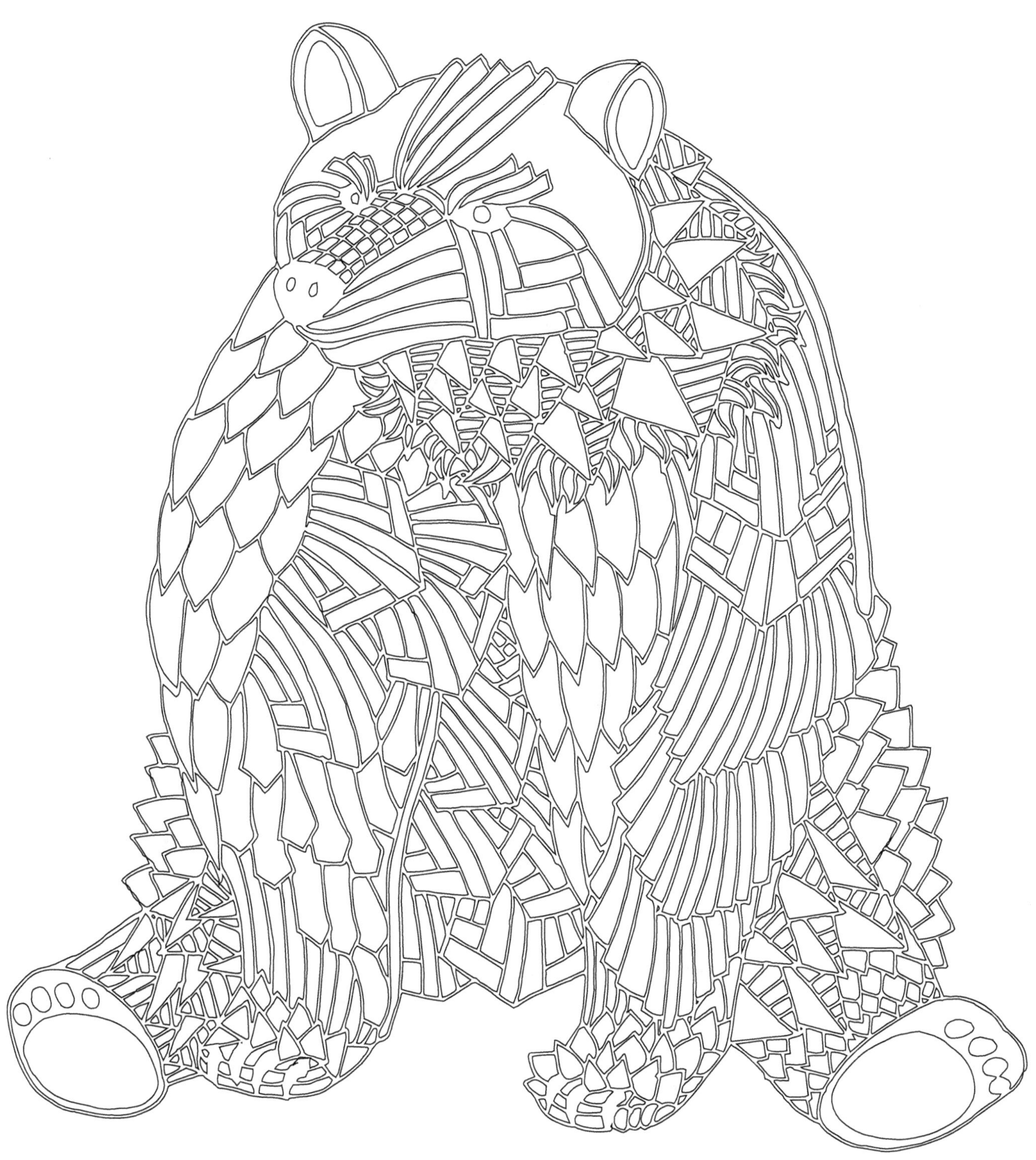

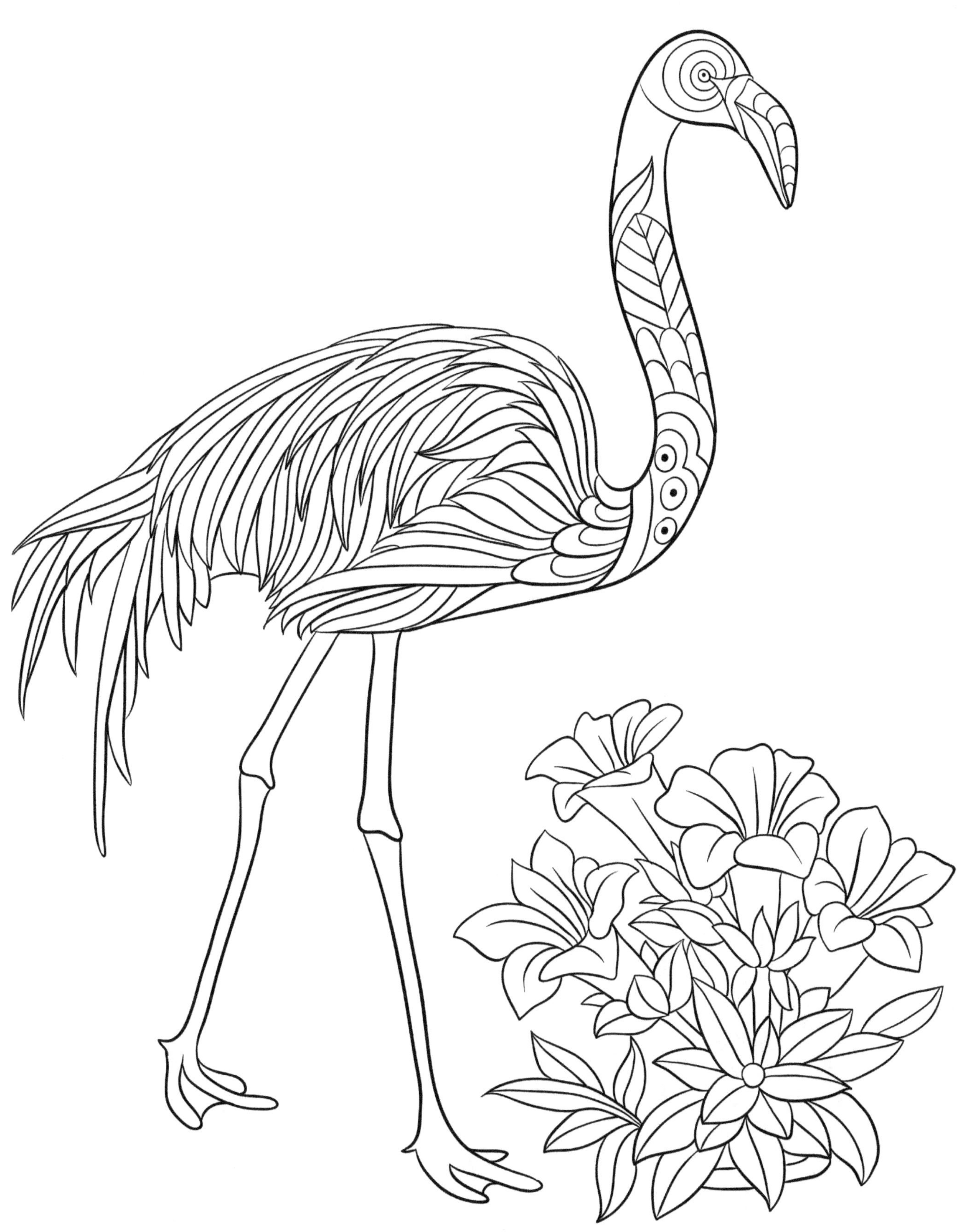

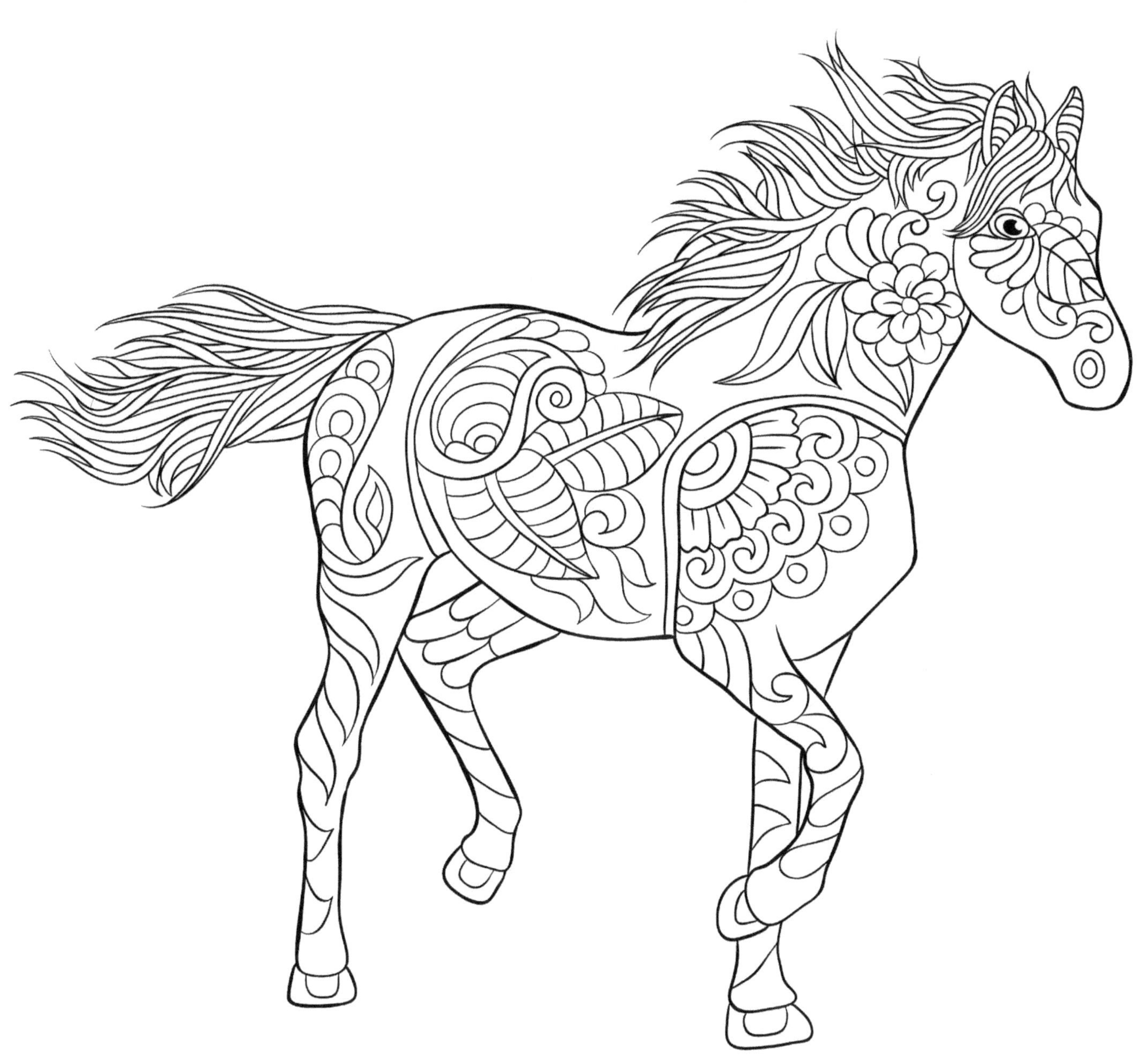

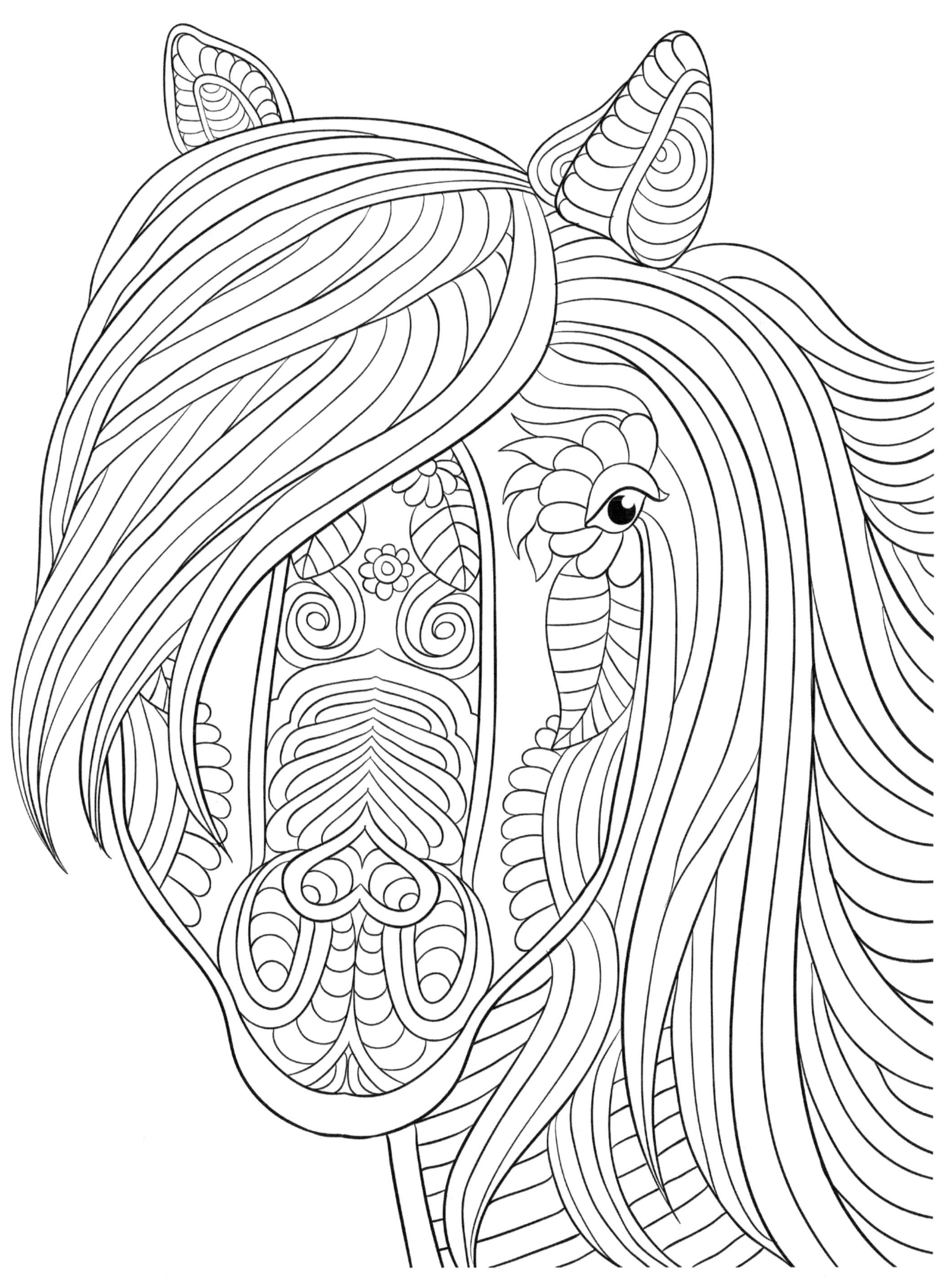

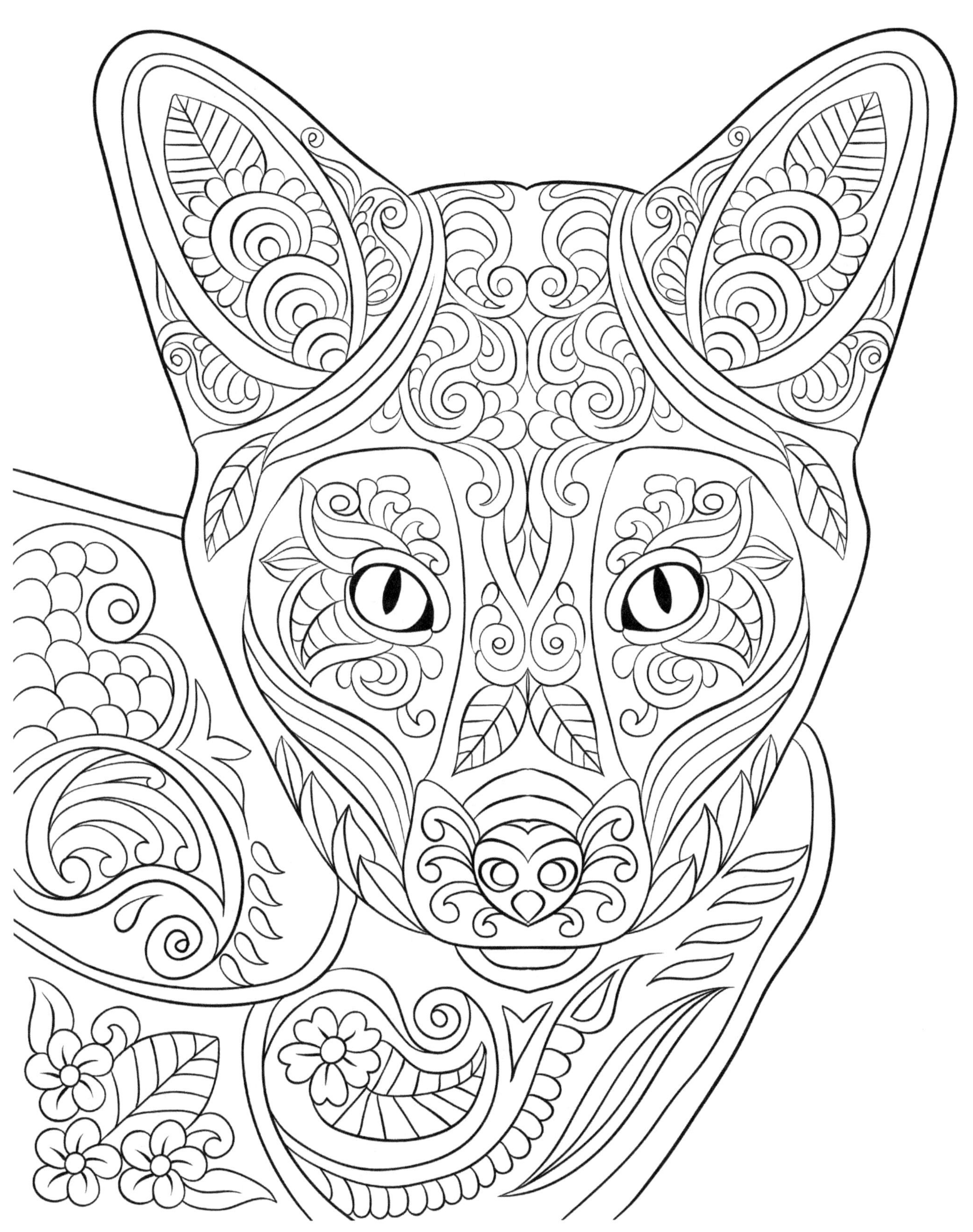

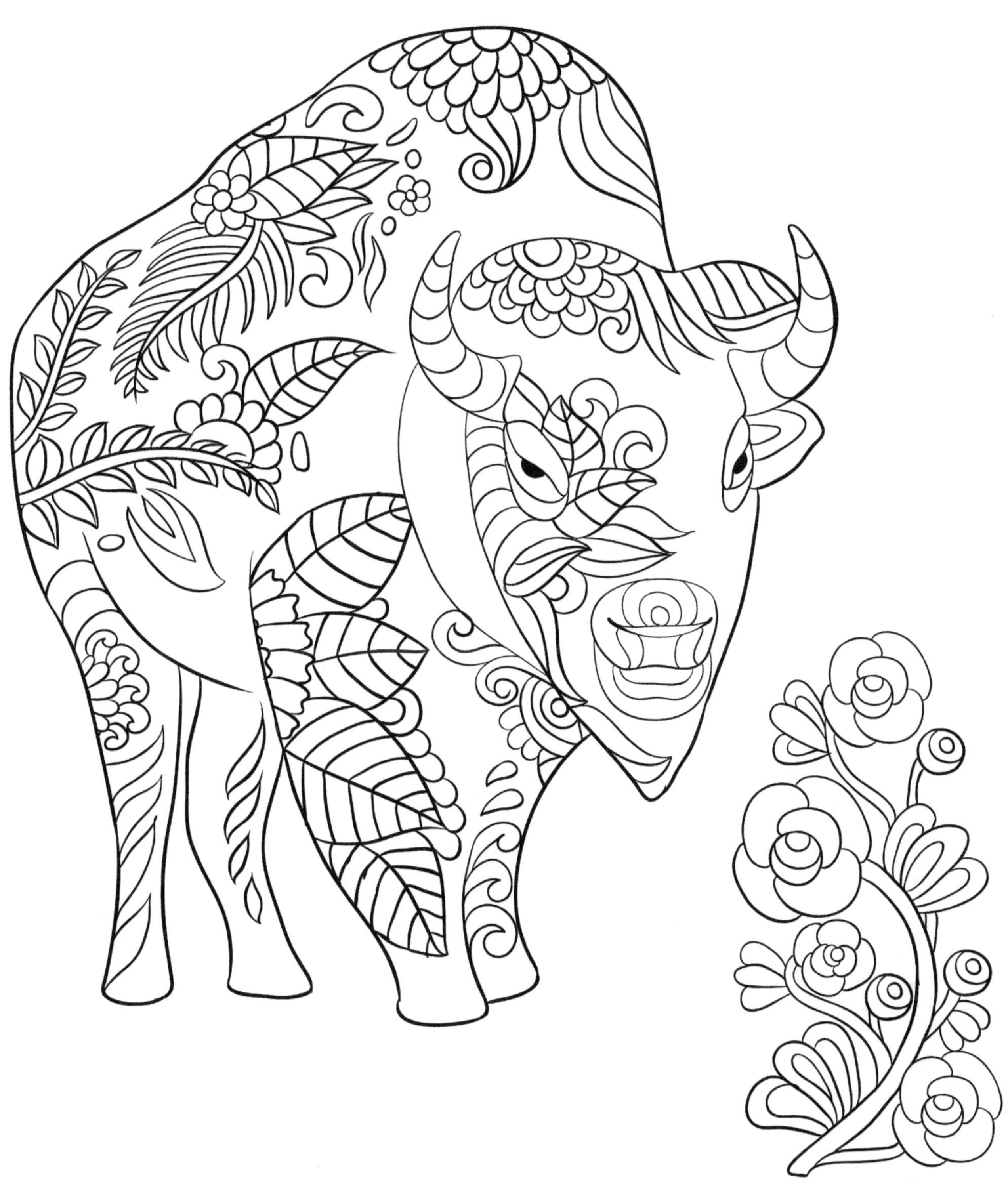

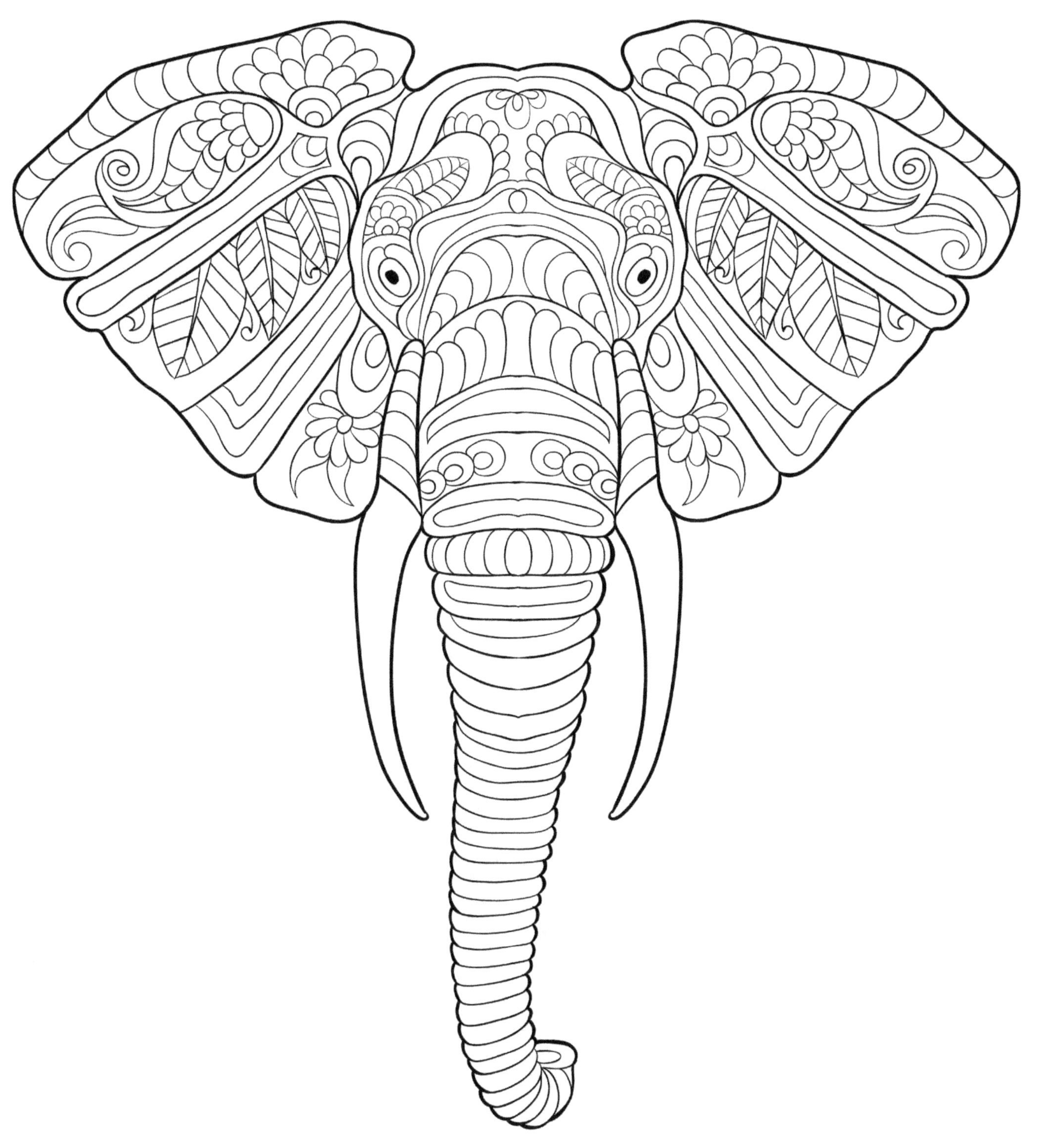

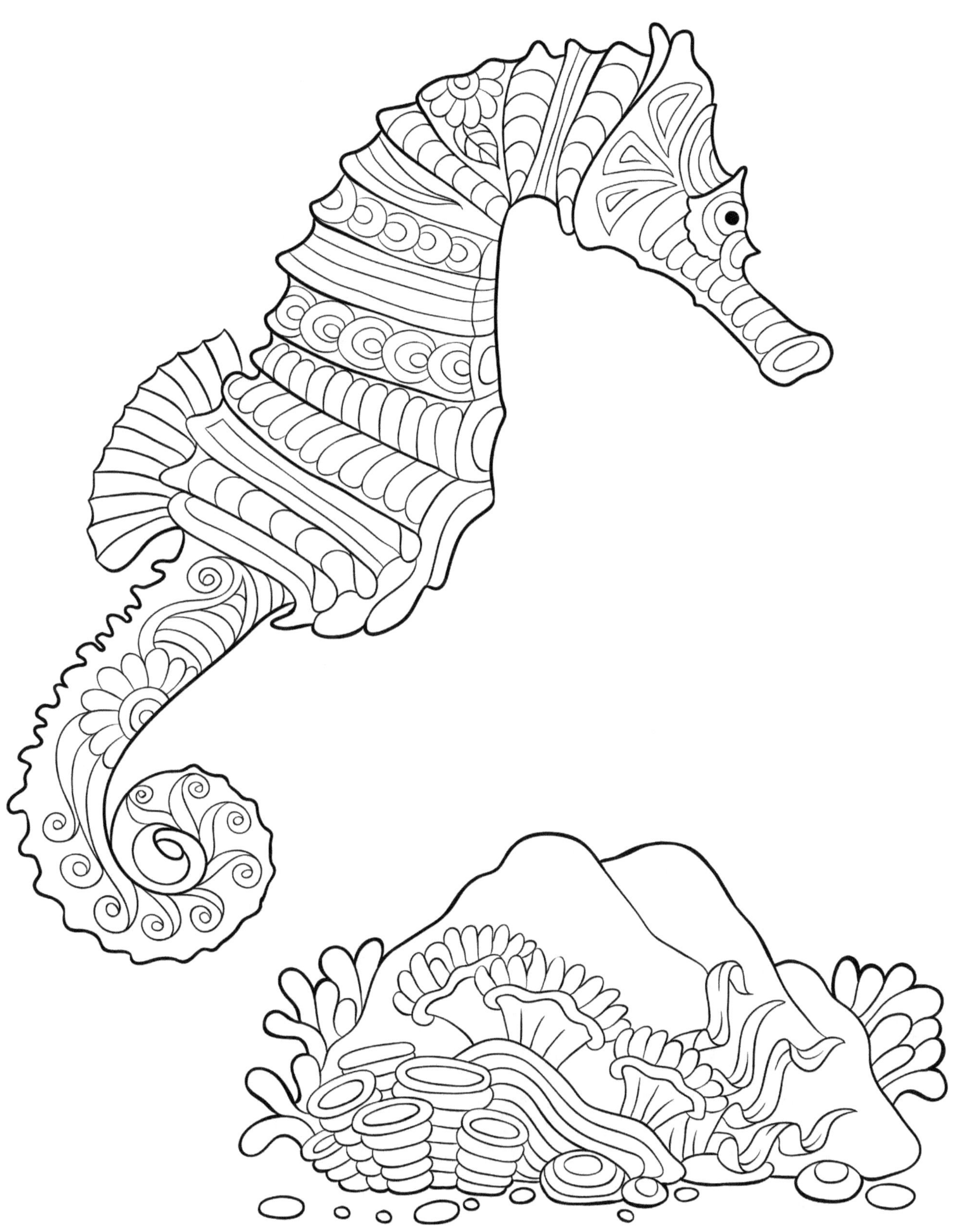

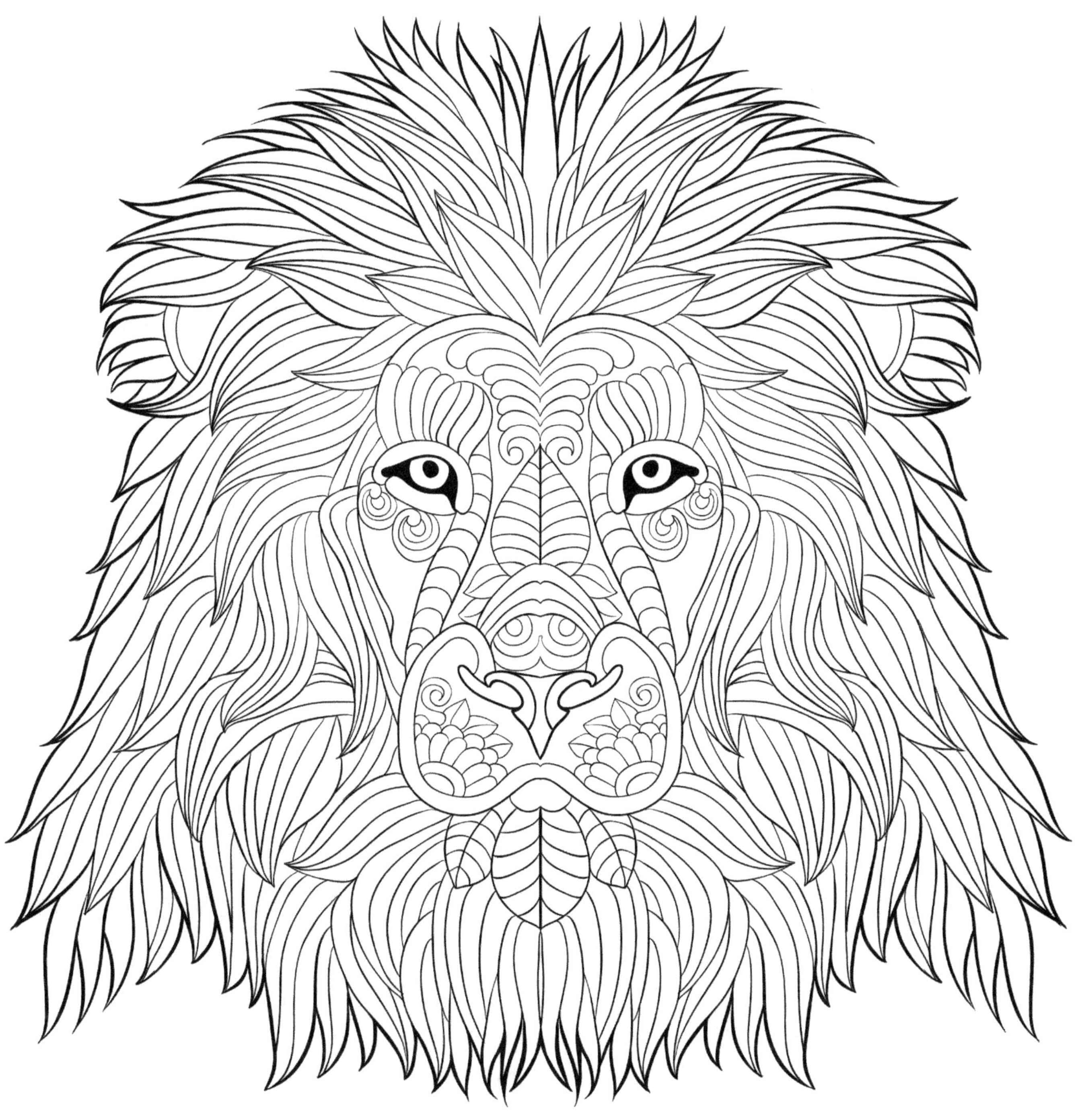

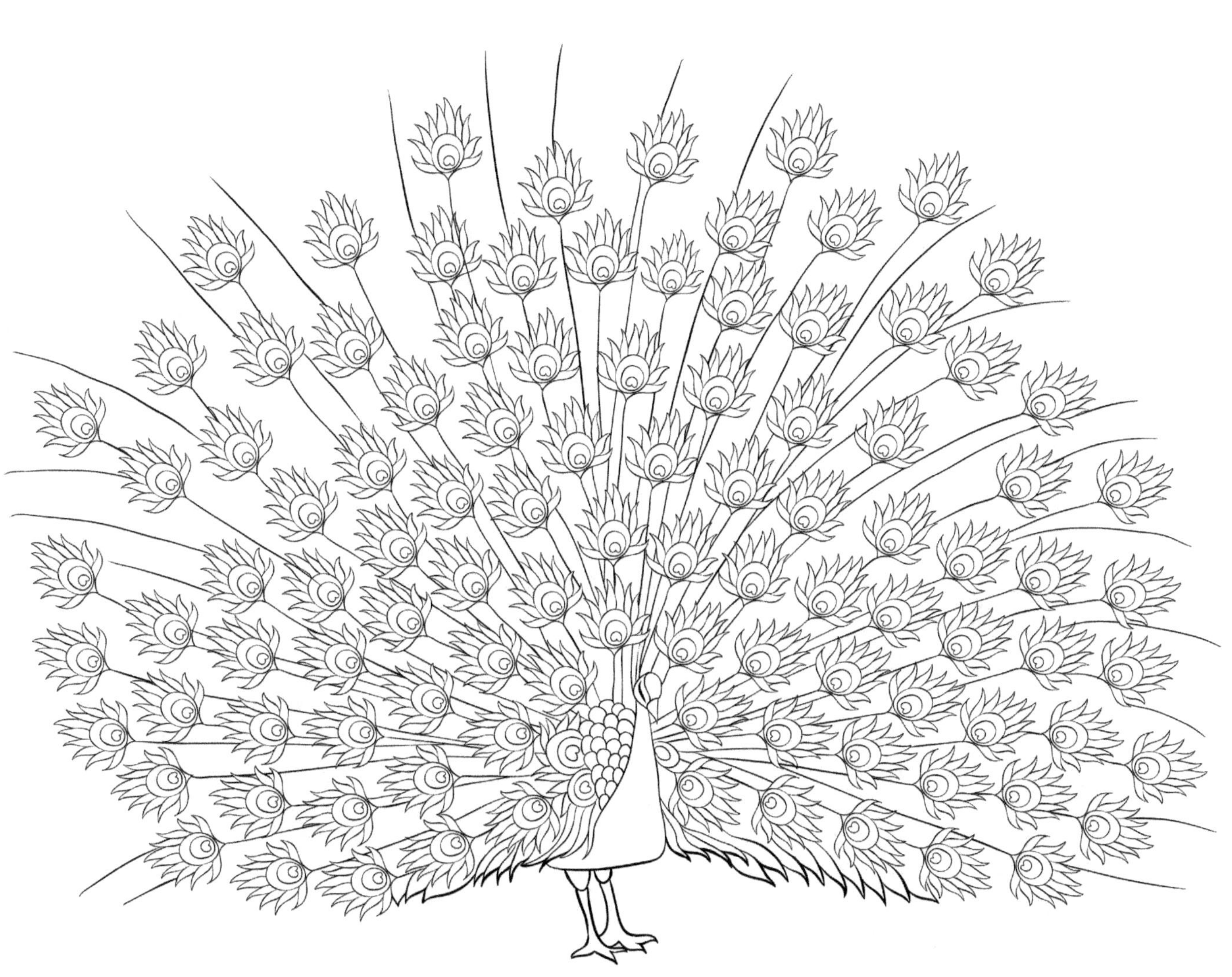

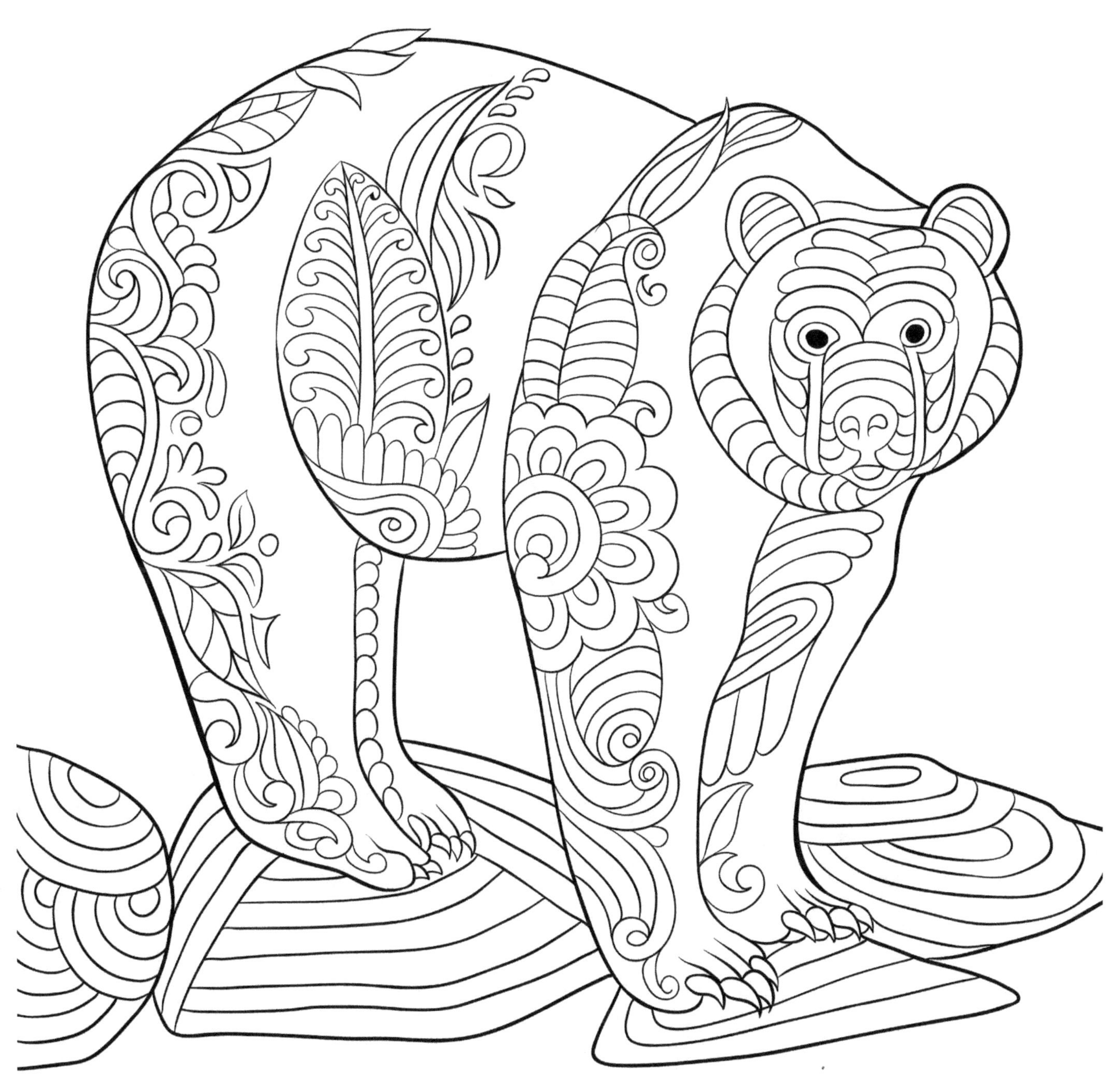

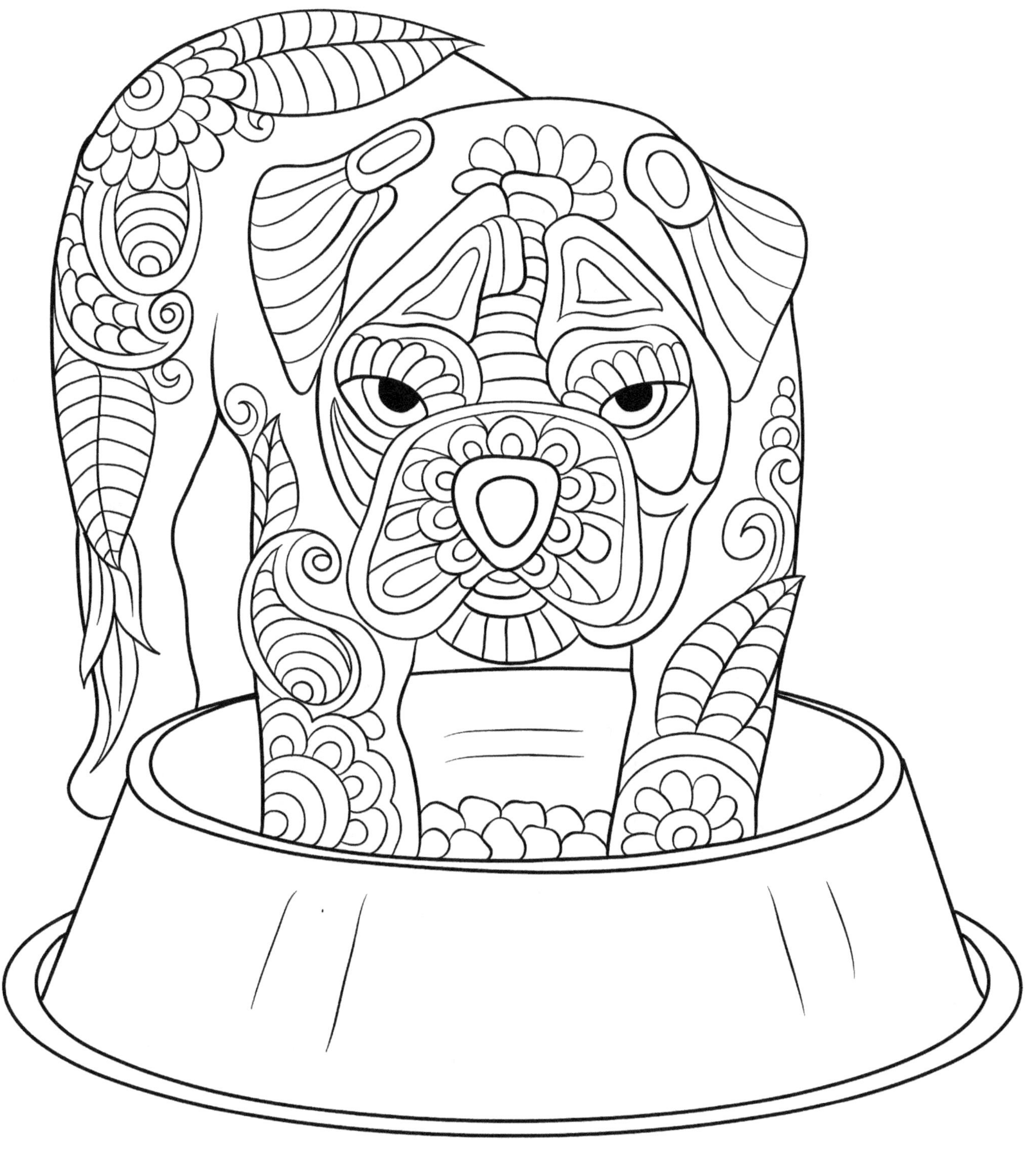

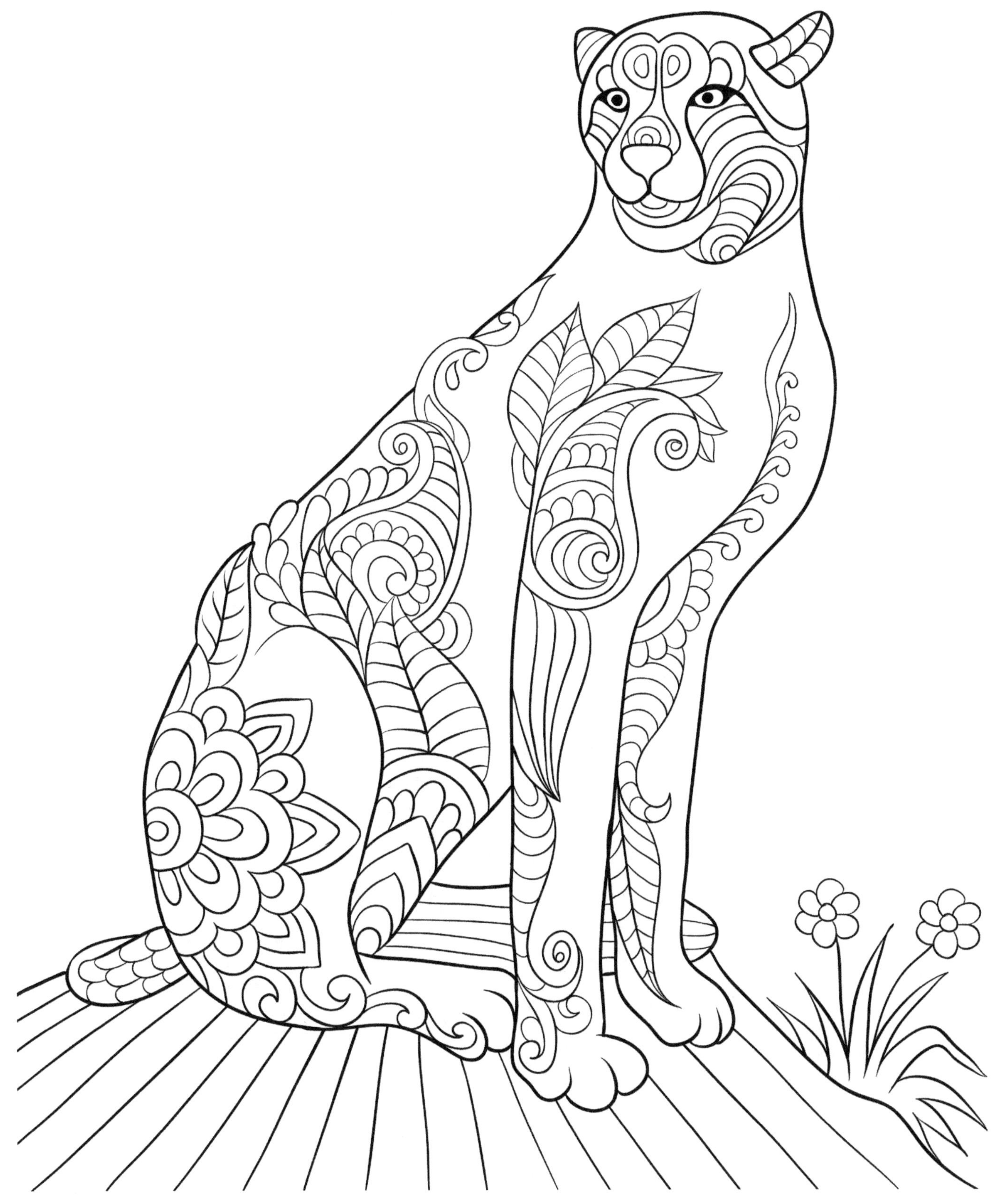

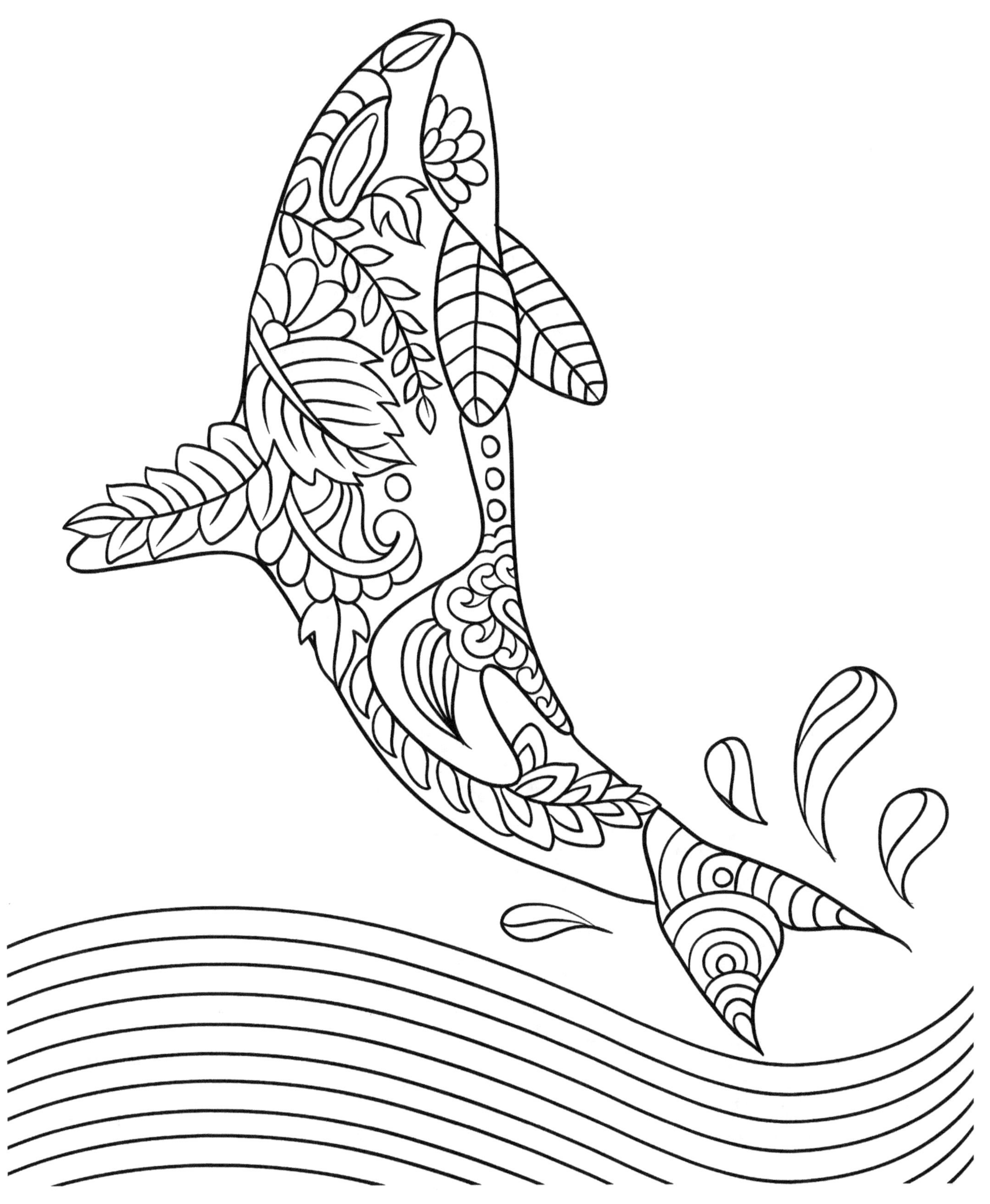

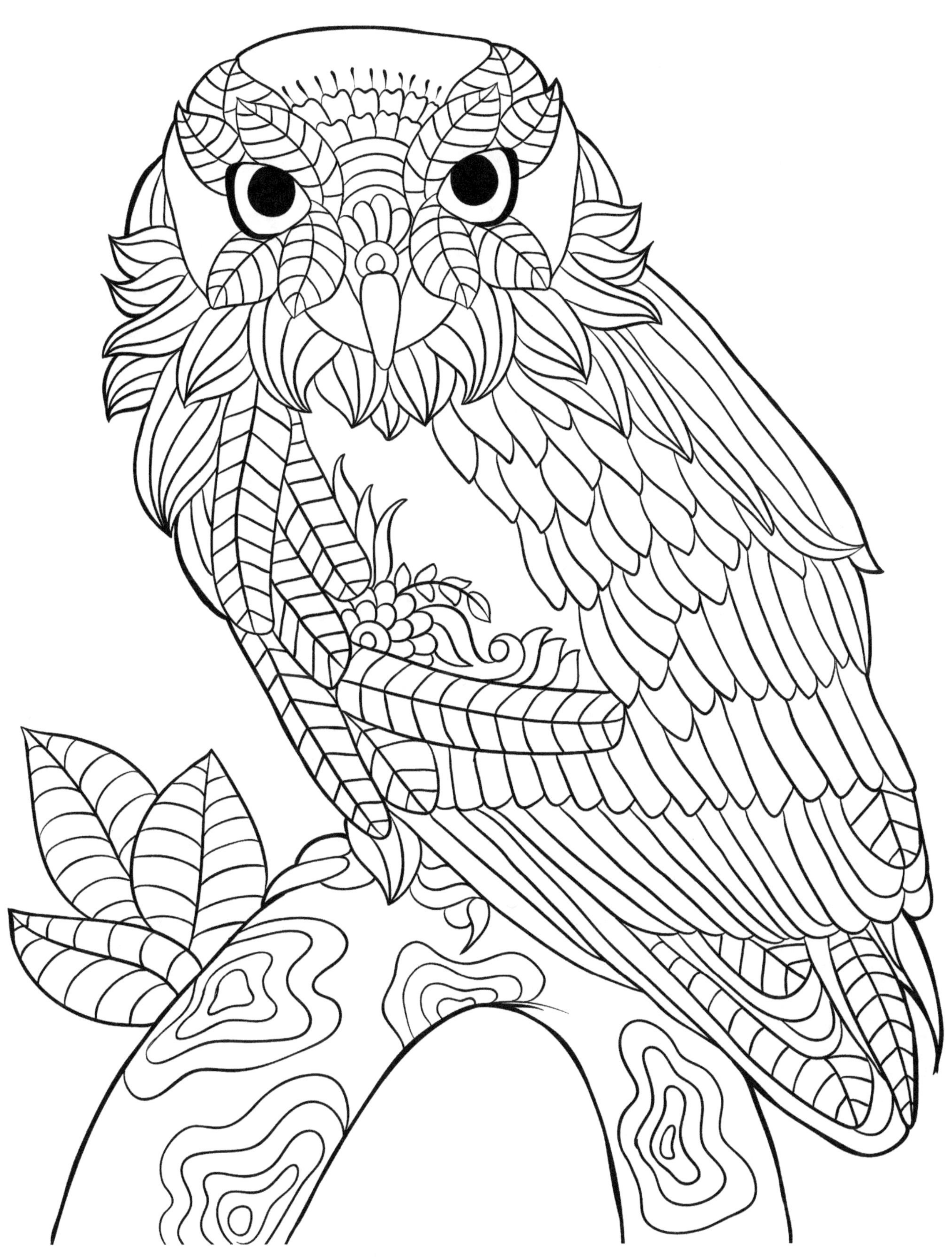

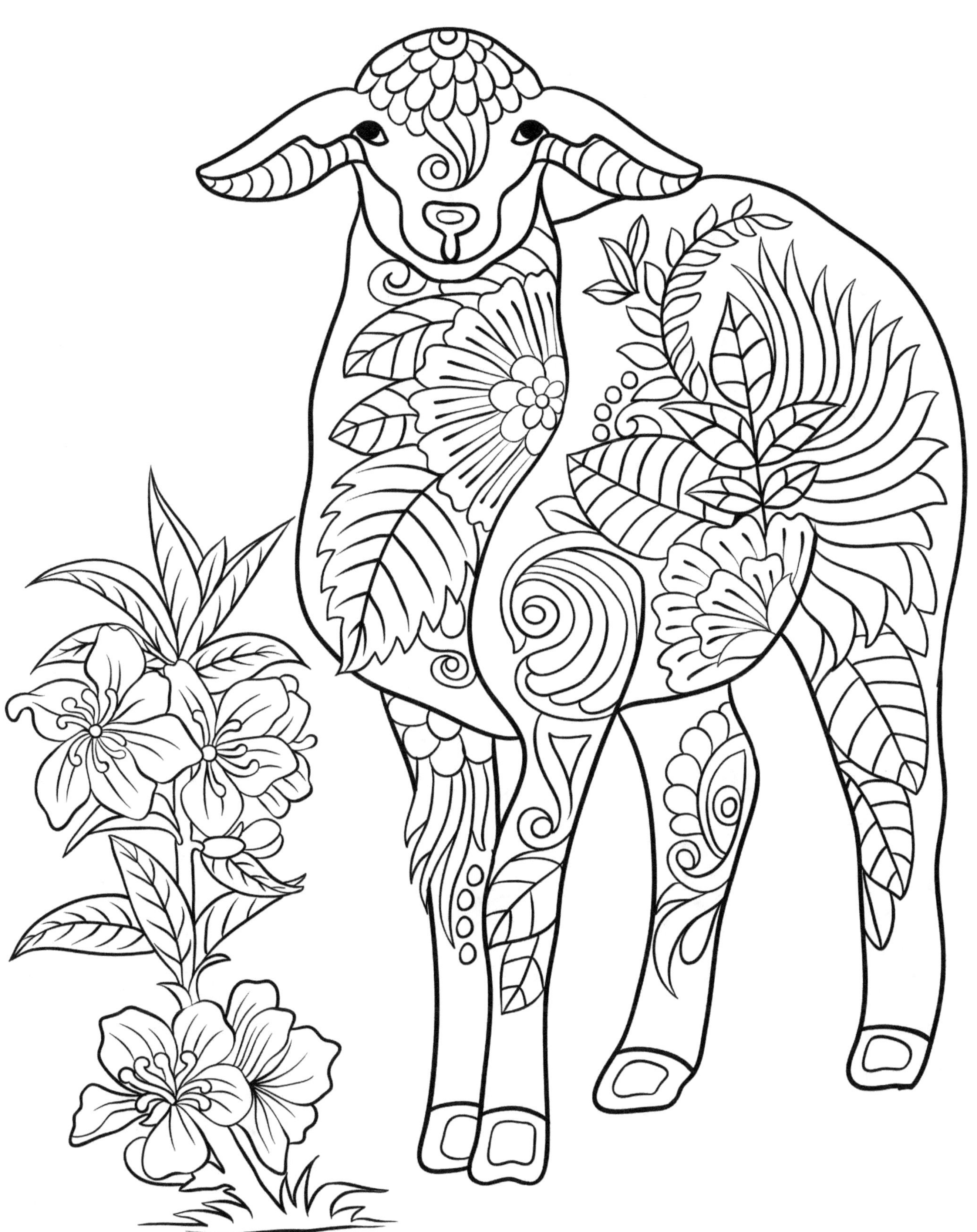

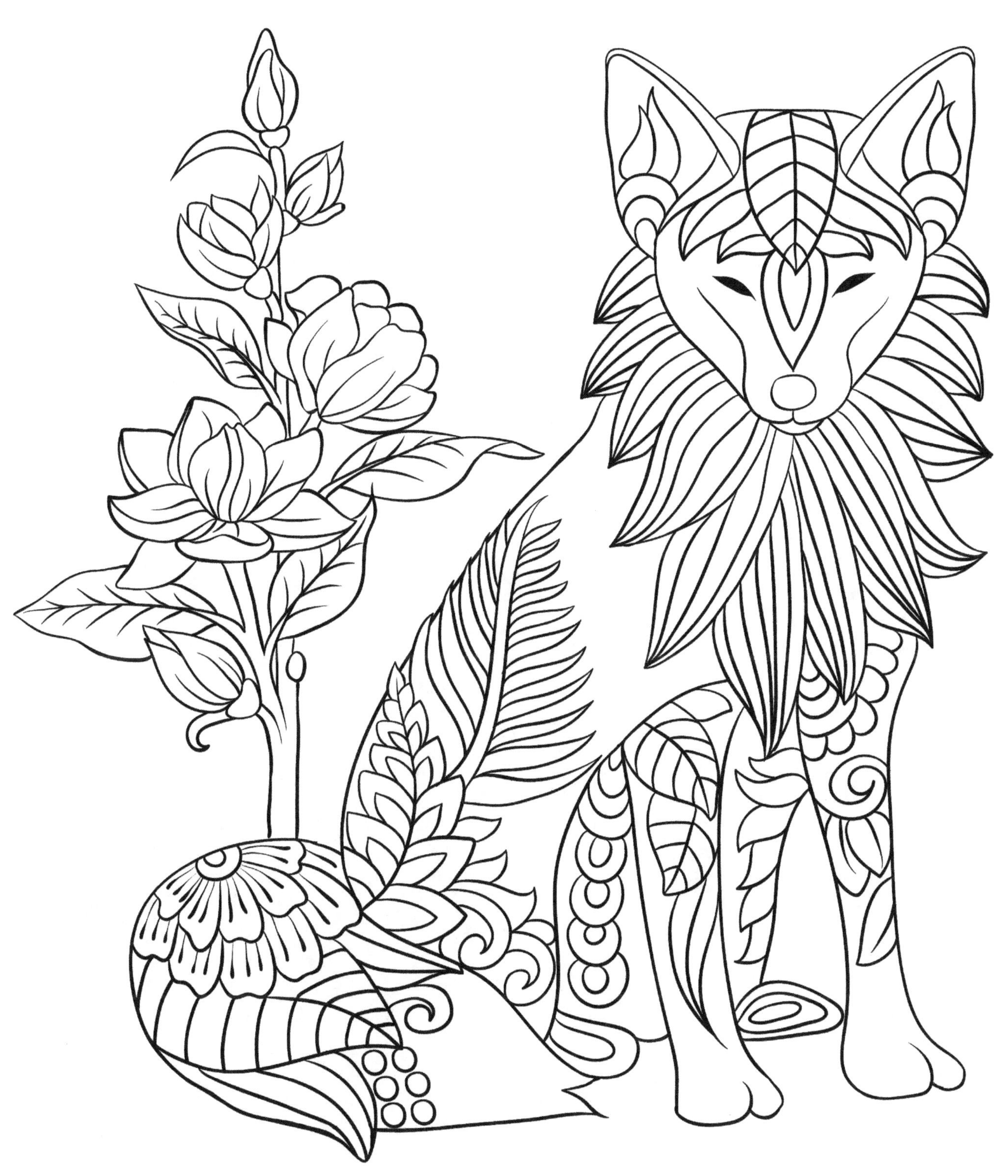

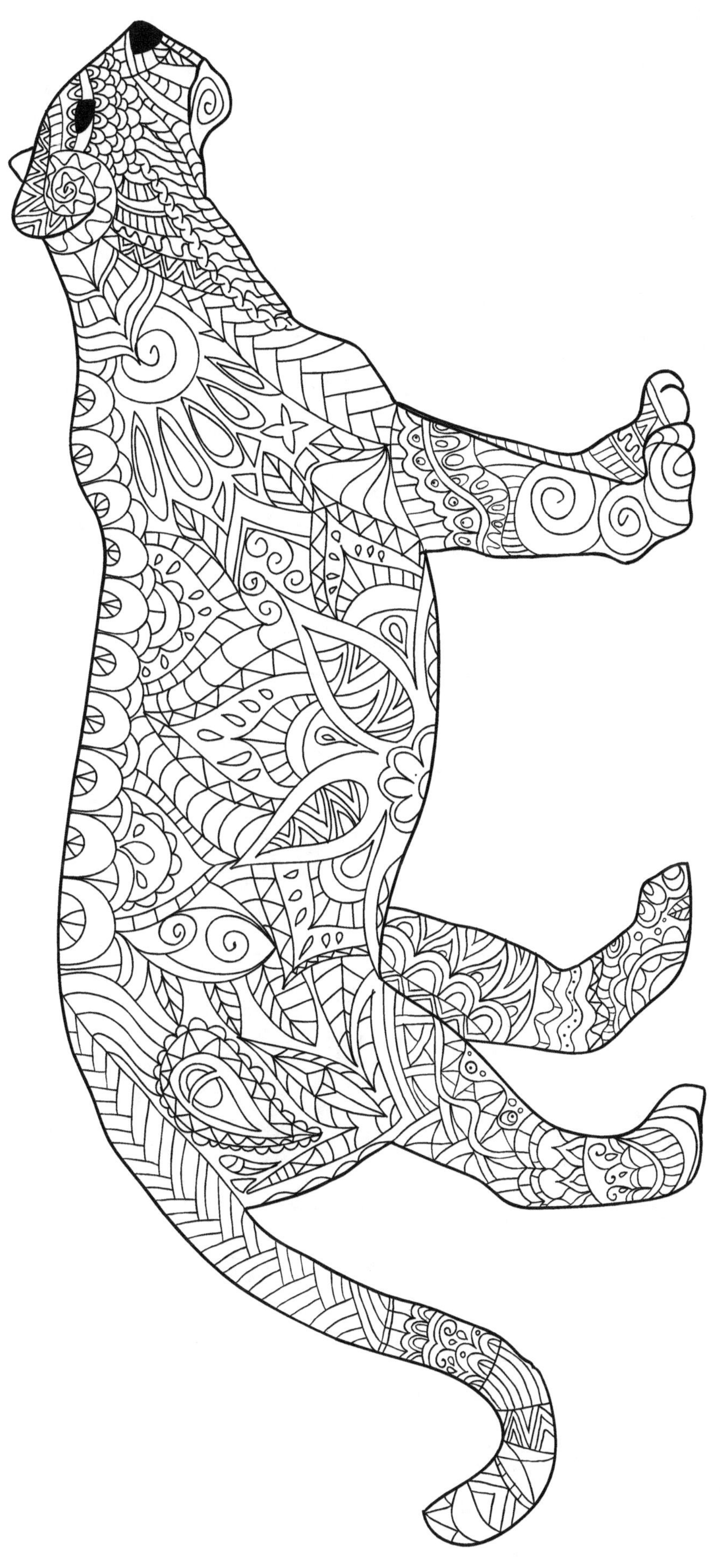

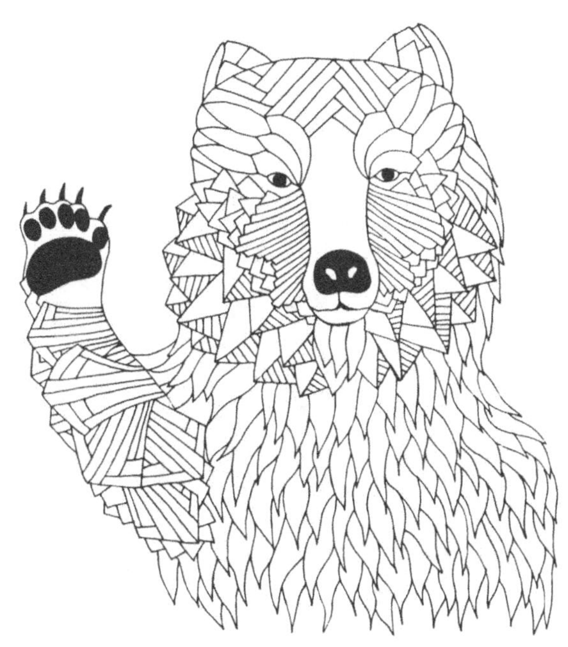

www.ingramcontent.com/pod-product-compliance
Lightning Source LLC
LaVergne TN
LVHW080334110826
845155LV00027B/240
* 9 7 8 1 9 3 9 0 0 8 0 1 5 *